THE LIVING ARE FEW, THE DEA ...

Eclectics & Heteroclites 13

HANS HENNY JAHNN

THE LIVING ARE FEW, THE DEAD MANY

Translated and introduced by Malcolm R. Green

ATLAS PRESS, LONDON

HANS HENNY JAHNN

ro
ro
ro

Ungeheure Geschichten

CONTENTS

Introduction ... 7

Kebad Kenya ... 21

Sassanid King ... 35

A Master Selects his Servant ... 57

The Night of Lead ... 83

Brief Autobiography ... 169

Published by Atlas Press,
27 Old Gloucester St., London WC1N 3XX.
Die Nacht aus Blei: ©1987 by Hoffmann und Campe Verlag, Hamburg.
Ein Herr wählt seinen Diener, Kebad Kenya, Sassanidischer König:
©1974 by Hoffmann und Campe Verlag, Hamburg.
Kleine Selbstbiographie: ©1974 by Hoffmann und Campe Verlag, Hamburg.
Translation ©2012, Atlas Press
Printed and bound by CPI Group (UK) Ltd., Croydon, CR0 4YY
A CIP record for this book is available from
The British Library.
ISBN: 1-900565-59-5
ISBN-13: 978-1-900565-59-2
USA distribution: ARTBOOK/D.A.P.
155 Sixth Avenue, 2nd Floor, New York, NY 10013
Tel: (212) 627-1999 Fax: (212) 627-9484.
UK distribution: TURNAROUND
www.turnaround-uk.com
orders@turnaround-uk.com

The translation of this work was supported by a grant from
the Goethe-Institut which is funded by the German Ministry of Foreign Affairs.

GOETHE-INSTITUT

INTRODUCTION

Writing about his earliest years, Hans Henny Jahnn (1894–1959) tells us: "My mother used to drag me along to a gravestone on which was inscribed: 'Here rests Hans Jahnn'." This was the grave of his older brother, who had died aged two, a year before Hans Henny was born. "That was one of the most terrible and decisive experiences of my childhood."[1] "It was one of the most appalling, truly satanic impressions I had to deal with as a child."[2] Jahnn came to believe he was loved only as an "ersatz child", not least because he thought himself repulsively ugly while his brother "had been a picture of beauty". He had seen his "own" grave before he had even properly embarked on life, and later felt he was being dragged down into it by his departed brother: "I was convinced that I bore his soul, a foreign soul that now was approaching its true body and wanted to enter it and the grave, to go straight to the grave."[3] Jahnn often returned to this event in his autobiographical writings, even in his sixties.[4] And yet the name of Jahnn's brother was Gustav Robert Jahn. Hans must have dreamt the story up, just as he added the second "n" to the family surname. His tendency to embellish his autobiography, along with his obsession and

1. Cited in *Geschichte der deutschen Literatur von 1945 bis zur Gegenwart*, ed. Wilfried Barner, Munich, 2006, 2nd edition, p.69.
2. Walter Muschg, *Gespräche mit Hans Henny Jahnn*, Frankfurt, 1966, p.59.
3. As for instance in Thomas Freeman, *Hans Henny Jahnn, eine Autobiographie*, Hamburg, 1974, p.34f.; Josef Winker, "Nachwort" in *Nacht aus Blei*; Jahnn, *Frühe Schriften*, Hamburg, 1993, p.530.
4. See Elsbeth Wolffheim's monograph, *Hans Henny Jahnn*, Reinbeck, 1989, p.133, note 7.

identification with death are two of those matters that were "withheld" in his "Brief Autobiography" (see the end of this book). Equally traumatic and just as shrouded in autobiographical myth are his schooldays. According to his own account, he suffered terribly at school, not least when a torrid religiosity gripped him. He never went anywhere without the New Testament in his pocket, and attempted to live without telling a single lie. This resulted in endless punishments and ostracism at school, and his family considered sending him to a mental institution. His religious frenzy coincided with the extreme inner struggles he experienced with his first sexual experiences, which in turn led to his abandoning Christianity and adopting a morality that embraced the contrary nature of man, both body and mind, at once a part of and outside nature.

Such beliefs opened a gulf between Jahnn and his increasingly nationalistic peers. Already a pacifist before the outbreak of World War One, he fled illegally into Norwegian exile with his close friend from school, Gottlieb Harms, until the war was over. On his return to Germany he had with him his first play, written, he claimed, in only four weeks: *Pastor Magnus Ephraim.* On publication in 1919 it received the much-coveted Kleist Prize and shortly afterwards was staged by Brecht. This precocious tale of a family's sexual and religious torments amid the collapse of Christian values, of sexual murder, self-castration and crucifixion, had a tempestuous reception. Another five plays followed in the years until his second exile in 1933. For some time Jahnn was known only as a playwright, but 1929 saw the publication of his first novel, *Perrudja* (from which the story "Sassanid King" is taken), which is nowadays considered one of his greatest literary achievements. Despite positive reviews from writers as prominent as Klaus Mann and Alfred Döblin, the work sold poorly. Fortunately he was able to support himself by means altogether different from literature, through church-organ building and restoration. He stumbled upon this field almost entirely by chance, and became its visionary, spearheading almost single-handedly the organ reform movement. By the time he left Germany in 1933, he had been involved in restoring at least 100 organs, and it is telling that the largest part of his "Brief Autobiography", written for a literary review, revolves around his achievements in this area.

It was also during the early years between the wars that Jahnn together with Harms and the sculptor Franz Busse founded an artists' community called the Ugrino Society — the *Glaubensgemeinschaft Ugrino*. It was registered as a "religious community" so that Jahnn, now in his mid-twenties, could realise some of his very specific ideas about burial, which could only be legally performed if they were backed by a religious organisation. The Ugrino burial rites specified that the body was to be laid out for a very long period, was to be kept intact, and to be buried in a coffin made of lead or zinc and sealed with wax. While the community was not religious in the usual meaning of the term, it did subscribe implicitly to an impersonal divine principle, expressed through a neo-Platonic system called "harmonics" based on the ideas of Johannes Kepler as well as the music theorist and speculative philosopher Hans Kayser. These principles were to be conveyed to the world through art, especially baroque music, writing and publishing, sculpture, theatre and sacred architecture, but the essence of Ugrino remained, according to Jahnn, impossible to grasp in words. It aimed at emancipating all that science, Christianity and technology had repressed — the sensual, physical, pre-linguistic side of human existence, and thus at healing the split of mind and body. The society held regular organ concerts in Hamburg, established a highly regarded publishing house for sheet music by rarely heard baroque and pre-baroque composers, and planned a series of mortuary buildings that reflected Jahnn's love of Egyptian and Romanesque monuments. Jahnn's attempts to raise the necessary finances were thwarted by a series of disastrous land speculations, and most of these building plans never came to fruition. The only notable exceptions were two small edifices designed by Jahnn: the first was a monument to his family based on harmonic principles drawn from the mediaeval French architect Villard de Honnecourt; the second was his own tomb.

The Society drifted apart in the latter half of the 1920s, in part it seems because of its rigid hierarchy and androcentricity. Whilst it shared many of the failings as well as the anti-rationalist stance of similar life-reform societies of the day, the Ugrino Society never evinced any nationalist tendencies. Quite the contrary, and Jahnn himself was convinced that the white race was utterly degenerate; what is more, as early as 1933 he had become a highly vociferous critic of the Fascist terror that was already establishing itself in Germany.

It is no surprise then that the rise of National Socialism in the early 1930s caused Jahnn to go into exile yet again, this time to the Danish island of Bornholm (from 1934 to 1950), where with the help of wealthy friends he managed to acquire a farm. He was accompanied by his wife Ellinor, a member of the Ugrino Society he had married in 1926, by their daughter Signe, and by the widow and son of Gottlieb Harms who had died in 1931. Apart from being excluded in 1938 from the *Reichsschrifttumkammer*, the writers' section of Goebbels' "Chamber of Culture", and being gradually edged out of the organ reform society, Jahnn was never actively persecuted by the National Socialists. He was as he put it "not banned, but not approved", and continued to be in contact with, and to make occasional visits to Germany, in part to tend to Harms' grave.

In Bornholm, Jahnn ran his farm largely from his desk, though he actively dedicated himself to one of his great loves, horses, and to writing, even if he had no possibilities of publishing during the war. He also embarked on the hormone research that was to occupy him until his death. These activities have often been cited in recent decades in support of Jahnn being a kind of proto-"Green". As a farmer he was vehemently against artificial fertilisers, or indeed any machinery in farming, and claimed from his hormone research that separating the dung of cows pregnant with heifers from that of those carrying bullocks could lead to "a 5 to 20 per cent increase" in yield for arable crops.[5] In this, as in much that he did, Jahnn saw himself as acting in accord with harmonic law, as well as with the agricultural systems of ancient Egypt and Babylon, whose cultures he admired enormously. He also claimed to have isolated a completely unknown hormone in mares' urine, which he called "miramon" and viewed as a universal palliative.[6]

This new word even crept into the pages of his four-part novel *Fluß ohne Ufer* (*River Without Banks*). The first volume appeared in 1949 just as Jahnn was returning to Germany, but while extensively reviewed, sales remained poor, as did those for volume two. Practical considerations might have prompted the publication of a popular-looking paperback with a somewhat salacious cover, *13 nicht geheure Geschichten* (*13 Uncanny Tales*), a

5. See Rolf Italiaander, *Hans Henny Jahnn, Aufzeichnungnen eines Einzelgängers*, Munich, 1959, p.12.
6. See Armin Schäfer, *Biopolitik des Wissens: Hans Henny Jahnns literarisches Archiv des Menschen*, Würzburg, 1996, p.149f.

collection of stories extracted from the novels *Perrudja* and *Fluß ohne Ufer* and from which the first three stories in the present volume are taken. The word *"geheuer"* (uncanny) had a particular meaning for Jahnn, who observed that "the normal person's instinctive censorship battles with the autonomous goal of all poetry, because everything to which he is not accustomed is uncanny".[7]

Jahnn's last decade was his most politically radical, when he took up issues which most would have thought strange, to say the least. He championed animal rights, and fought Adenauer's plans for German rearmament and the deployment of nuclear energy. He was way ahead of his time when already, in 1956, his tract *Der Mensch im Atomzeitalter* noted that "All attempts to dispose of nuclear waste have proven until now to be inadequate", that nuclear energy could cause genetic damage, and that the next World War could only be nuclear.

Central to Jahnn's literary work was his fixation on the embrace of death and sexuality, decay and eroticism. His early sexual awakening was clearly homosexual: he fell in love with Gottlieb Harms at school, and it was doubtless his homosexual urges that cast Jahnn into such religious turmoil. He and Harms must have resolved the practicalities of this relationship by the time they left for Norway in 1914; it came to an end only after several years, and following a lengthy *ménage à trois* with Jahnn's future wife, Ellinor Philips. However, Jahnn and Harms remained close until the latter's untimely death. Both of them had by then entered into conventional marriages and had children, in Jahnn's case with Ellinor, with whom he fell in love "at first sight". She was very much a free spirit and

7. See Italiaander, *op. cit.*, p.7.

openly accepted Jahnn's affairs with both men and women. Jahnn wrote of her in 1954: "Not only did I idolise her then, I love her to this day".

Jahnn's life as an active bisexual has proved inconvenient for those who have tried to style him as a "gay writer".[8] As in most aspects of his life, he eluded conventional tags, and in a conversation with Hubert Fichte he claimed to be "omnisexual".[9] When the question of Jahnn's sexuality is critically examined, attempts to construe such central images as the mare or the angel of death (who appears here in every story but one) as ciphers for homosexuality do not really convince. Whereas the charged atmosphere of *The Night of Lead* might be partly explained by its homo-sexual content, this does not explain the sense of guilt and doom that accompanies it here and elsewhere in Jahnn's œuvre. Jahnn's homoerotic world is more sinful and guilt-ridden than, for instance, that of Genet (whom he read) and lacks the unencumbered innocence of the mares he perhaps would have liked to emulate. Nor do such reductive readings account for the entanglements of identity, of fraternal worship, of self-mirrored and self-split identities that suffuse the poetry of these narratives. Any single interpretation seems contrary to Jahnn's intentions and introduces normative, non-harmonic restrictions that are exactly what he sought to resist.

In fact Jahnn appears to have deliberately smudged the edges of his narratives so as to make direct understanding almost impossible. One example of this is to be found in *The Night of Lead*, originally a sequence

8. See for instance *Die Suche nach dem rechten Mann*, edited by Wolfgang Popp, Berlin, 1984, which attempts to demonstrate that Jahnn's prose is not simply homoerotic but homo*sexual*. Cf. also the openly gay writer Josef Winkler's postface to *Die Nacht aus Blei*.

9. Cited in Freeman, *op. cit.*, pp.553, 637.

extracted from a much longer novel that was never finished, *Jeden ereilt es* (*It comes to us all*). The reader may well be baffled by the word "Gari" that occurs in two places in the piece, tremulously declaimed by Matthieu, the main character. Who or what is "Gari"? No explanation is offered, and Gari has been viewed as some kind of *deus ex machina* who is observing or precipitating the unfolding action, or as an incarnation of the angel of death (and here given the Yiddish name of *Malach Ha-Mavis*). But if we consult the text of which it was a part, Gari turns out to be a sailor and Matthieu's lover. Evidently the ragged edges left by tearing this piece out of its context were unimportant to Jahnn, and ambiguities around events, time and place, and even syntax always suffused his writings.

Even today Jahnn presents the reader with a very original reading experience, because he is more concerned with cosmic events, suprahuman occurrences redolent with harmonics, rather than with something as pedestrian as psychology. The larger landscape of his novels resembles that of several of his contemporaries such as Hermann Broch or Alfred Döblin, along with many of the Expressionists — he avoided psychological motivations and development, and concentrated instead on an atemporal progression. Characters for Jahnn are the "arena for musically expressed events, for themes, stanzas, motifs, echoes and rhythms," as he wrote in a letter to his fellow author Werner Helwig in 1946 — a statement he often repeated. Even when emotions are described with clarity and precision, the disregard Jahnn shows for any sort of logical continuity can be startling, In *The Night of Lead* seemingly contradictory emotions follow one another in staccato cadences. The idea that Jahnn's works have a "symphonic" structure has often been proposed, but Jahnn loved baroque music above all, barely tolerated Mozart, and was dismissive of musical traditions such as Classicism and the Romantics that bolstered the bourgeois notion of the individual as a self set on a pedestal, with all its attendant psychologies. Instead, it was not Jahnn the rationalist, the Egyptian seer who was in charge, but Jahnn the berserker. His inner spirit expressed itself in a direct if ruder language than that of his mathematical theories. Thus, even when he spent weeks of research on a text such as "Sassanid King", the result is not something distanced and balanced but a writing forged with the breathless passion we encounter throughout Jahnn's œuvre as a whole.

Jahnn is reputed to have been stylistically influenced by modern experimentalists such as Joyce, but where Joyce's modernism was classical in form, the syntax essentially conventional, Jahnn reads at times almost as if he were writing automatic poetry. Utterly disparate elements tumble across his pages — baroque formulations, obscure words, slang, dialect, ungainly hybrid images, neologisms, reiteration, Old Testament sonorities, so much so that occasionally he has simply been dismissed as a "bad" writer.[10] Jahnn was humble enough to confess to Walter Muschg that he was unable to write smoothly, that he had to fight off appalling inhibitions with every line he wrote, that a number of sentences in *Perrudja* had brought him to the verge of suicide, and that after rewriting the opening sentence of the book at least fifty times, turning it forever back and forth, he simply contented himself with: "Perrudja ate his evening meal." He was being disingenuous, because his diaries are written in nice, conventionally flowing sentences. In his novels and plays he cultivated an artificial language, with the aim — as he noted in a diary entry from early 1915

10. For instance Wolfgang von Wangenheim in *"Die Unwahrheit meines Erzählens"*, *Schreibheft*, vol. 26, Essen, 1986, pp.161-3.

entitled "The Struggle" — that every possibility of language was to be marshalled in order to proclaim the absolute necessity of resisting the consensual power of facticity. Jahnn often did not express what he wanted to convey on a "word to fact" basis, but created instead swathes of words that say everything at once. Viewed in detail, his prose appears not only eccentric but even in places at odds with his intentions, which presents the translator with obvious problems. His overall expressive power is in part a result of the occasional grammatical awkwardness, his rhetorical idiosyncrasies, which must, for accuracy's sake, be retained.

This is a literature of intensities rather than description, one that is unconcerned with psychological acuity but with a world in which humankind is not so important and the human individual no more than vanity, nothing but the skin-deep cosmetic layer we encounter several times in the present book.

It was in his last years in Hamburg that Jahnn fixed his ultimate argument for depersonalising his writing to the extent we find in *The Night of Lead*: the belief that the inner springs of human action were simply glandular secretions. His hormone research came to dominate his thinking and led to a kind of scientific determinism which was perhaps the logical culmination of his anti-psychological approach, but appears ironic for this extraordinary personality with his vivid subjective powers of expression.

There are many paradoxes of this order in Jahnn's life: the pacifist who produced some of the last century's most violent prose; the man who believed in a higher order of mathematics and simultaneously in the powers of providence and angels of an almost picture-book naivety; a writer who seemed to revel in perversion, but who longed for sexual innocence; and the man who feared death and yet wrote constantly about his longing for it, as we also find in most of the stories collected here. Jahnn's death in 1959 was the result of heart problems. As he had ordained, he was buried in the grave he had designed, next to the sweetheart of his youth, Gottlieb Harms, and later his wife Ellinor, in a metal coffin according to the principles of Ugrino. The writer Hans Erich Nossack, who gave the funeral oration, recalled that the coffin was so heavy that the pallbearers had to stop and place it on the ground three times to rest as they carried its leaden bulk to the grave.

Jahnn was perhaps too peculiar a writer to have had direct literary followers, yet his influence has manifested itself in other ways. While various groups have attempted to sign him up to their socio-political agendas, his real influence has been performative. *The Night of Lead*, by far his best-known work, has been used for at least four musical compositions: by Hans-Jürgen von Bose (1981), Jakob Diehl (2008), Asmith Tietchens (1995) and Walter Ulbricht (1994); for three major choreographies: Heinz Spoerli in Basel (1985), Pierre Wyss in Wiesbaden (1991) and William Forsythe in Berlin (1981); and probably half a dozen on smaller stages. Von Bose has also made a musical adaptation of Jahnn's play *Medea* (1993) and Matthias Pintscher one of *Music from Thomas Chatterton* (1998), while most recently Detlef Glanert's opera of *Das Holzschiff* has been performed (2010, staged by Hans Kresnik). All of this says much about the impact Jahnn has had on his readers, as does another curious fact: with the exception of the *13 Uncanny Tales*, every single anthology that has appeared since his death has included, along with literary works, articles and essays on topics as various as nuclear warfare, organ-building, animal rights and so forth. The impression Jahnn has left is not simply that of a unique and powerful literary figure, but of someone involved in all aspects of life itself. Such had always been his intention.

The Living Are Few, The Dead Many*

*Hindu saying, and the epigraph to *Fluß ohne Ufer*.

Kebad Kenya

Kebad Kenya contemplated consuming the flesh of his own thighs. Raw, it hung down, still warm and pulsating with the blood from his heart; but already separated from the man it had belonged to and ready to grow back somewhere else. Or to rot away as pus. Kebad Kenya had swung himself up on to the back of his mare an hour before midnight. Not a star in the sky. No moon hidden behind the clouds. Neither path nor field lay before them. No gorge into which they could have plunged, no pond in which they could have drowned, no forest in which they could have strayed. They could not lose themselves, nor meet with disaster, because Kebad Kenya wanted the end; but it had yet to come. And since it was still not the end, but only darkness, within and without, he had to do something. He had to commit the sin or exhaust himself. Yet he resisted the sin, as enticing as it had so often seemed and seemed so once again. Formerly he had plunged into it, been ground down by it as if between two millstones; but now the hatred with which he had yielded to it had grown feeble; even this adversary, thirsting for a victim, was beset by weakness. So one alternative alone remained — to exhaust himself. He rode off between the two darknesses and flayed his thighs to shreds, up to his belly. And the horse's back became as raw and bloody as his own skin. Had the night not ended, if the sun had tarried and risen a day later, he would have grown into the back of the horse. The animal's heart and his human heart would have poured their sap together into the hideous brotherhood of a hybrid, a hippocentaur.

Kebad Kenya had wished it thus in order to be freed of his guilt, but the sun lit up the eastern sky. The rider halted before his house and contemplated consuming the flesh of his thighs. He dismounted with difficulty, and looked at the lacerated mare. Tears welled up in his eyes. He lamented: "Oh!" he cried into the animal's ear, "I am damned. But there must be an end to me." He entered the house and dispatched his servants to fetch the neighbours. He lay down on his bed as if smitten by weakness. It was a ploy. He wanted to lure death. The neighbours came and gathered round the bed. No one asked him how he was. Or whether they could help him. They feared him and loathed him. For he was powerful, more powerful than all of them. He had a large house and many servants, but he kept them at a distance, like pigs in a sty. Rarely did he summon one of them. And when he did, it was bad for the one who was called.

"I have asked you to come," Kebad Kenya began, "for my condition is grave. I have neither wife nor child, nor friends, but you are my neighbours. Maybe you are not to be trusted, but nevertheless you are preferable to my servants, whom I would like to slay. Yet I have never slain a servant, even if people say I have. So even if I am innocent of this sin, as too other sins which you, my neighbours, commit daily, still I have sinned in another way. If it would help to wail about it and fill myself with remorse, then I would do so. Were it to God's liking, I would even do it for His sake. But how can He find delight in my pitiful voice? How can He find the leisure to listen to me repeating my lapses, which He already knows? For this reason I choose to remain unrepentant, because words can change nothing of my guilt."

The neighbours were appalled and cried: "This blasphemy against God is the greatest sin of all!" But he continued calmly: "My house, my land, my forests and the banks of my brooks shall belong to you, for you are my neighbours. I could be generous to my servants, whom I have despised and tormented long enough. But they are even less trustworthy than you. Therefore I shall not consider bestowing my property on them."

The neighbours then replied: "If this is what is in the depths of your heart, we shall try to assist you. Knowing you as we do, you will not give away your riches without demanding something in return. So tell us what you require of us."

"It is as you surmise," Kebad Kenya commenced anew. "You know me slightly and are aware that I am capable of burning down my house, laying waste to my forests, scattering salt on my fields, and burying my money where none can find it. However, everything now is safe and sound. I have drawn up a list, and the list indicates what is to pass to each of my neighbours once I am dead and buried. So that no disputes shall arise. As far as it is in the power of man, I have tried to divide everything fairly."

"Tell us your conditions," they cried.

"Between the forests, where the four winds meet, lies a desolate clearing. The soil is barren and rocky; only juniper, holly and heather grow there. The taller trees don't dare approach. This clearing shall belong to no one. It is to remain my own. I wish to be carried there with my sin. For I come from a great solitude which I shared with the animals, and wish for a still greater one which I shall share with no one. It was this great solitude that was my sin, the greater one shall be my redemption. Until now I have spent my days on the back of a horse. Up there I shall no longer ride, if heaven's grace has not completely forsaken me. Therefore you must slay my mare in her stable, now, this next hour; and take her to the knacker's."

The neighbours were more appalled than ever. But they made no response. Tears flowed down Kebad Kenya's cheeks after these last words. He continued with effort: "It has to be. I need the greater solitude. But my blood is dangerous. It is inclined to break loose. Therefore you must wall me in, and with sturdy walls. Here are my conditions: you, my neighbours, must build an oak coffin, very narrow, very slender, but strong. The boards must be fastened together with large, tempered nails. Then carry me to the stony heath. Break a hole in the earth, and line the bottom, the walls, and, — once I have been lowered inside — the roof with stones and lime."

He fell silent and they quickly promised to carry out his wishes. Their fear of him was great, their greed to divide his property among them greater. They realised that he himself had shown them the best way to become completely free of him. However miserly they might be, they would spare neither lime nor stones.

Before dismissing them Kebad Kenya said: "The evil in me is strong." They nodded their heads, accepted that there was nothing more to be discussed, went out to the stable and slew the horse. Then they returned to their free-holdings and waited for the announcement of Kebad Kenya's death. And one or other of them prowled around his house, questioning the servants to make sure they did not miss the vital hour. They had the coffin made so as to be properly prepared. They dug a hole in the stony soil on the heath. They used twenty horses to bring up jagged square-stones and lime slaked with milk. Finally they placed the finished coffin in Kebad Kenya's abode so that he would know that they were respecting the contract and it was now for him to take the next step. And die. However, death did not wish to enter Kebad Kenya's house. Gradually he realised that taking to his bed with putrefying thighs was too feeble a ploy. Although he had given up food and drink, he was overcome by the fear that the temptations of his sin might lure him once again from his redemption. His defiance welled up and wanted to deny that his mare had been slain. He gave the order to have her led from the stable to his room. He had straw piled up for her beside his bed. Yellow oats lay in a trough. The servants he had given the orders to began to tremble from head to toe, but however horror-struck they were, they failed to respond. So Kebad Kenya redoubled his cunning. He closed his mouth and his eyes. He made himself motionless. He defied his chest to rise or fall. He became rigid — and a murmur went through the house. A portrait was taken from the wall, and carried out. It was said to be of the man who had fathered Kebad Kenya. Someone pulled the purse out from under his head, and a few coins rolled across the floor. Kebad Kenya wanted to leap up and punish the servants' dishonesty. But he forced himself to judge no more, for he had already judged himself. Finally he decided to die without the assistance of death. The effort of becoming motionless and growing cold demanded all his inner concentration and strength. Ultimately he had to reach the point of not hearing nor seeing, not even the light between his lashes. He still had a long way to go, and it was still not yet decided whether he would attain his goal when death so obviously refused him its aid. To his relief, the neighbours came earlier than he had anticipated. They shoved the coffin, which earlier they had placed in his house, into his room. The straw Kebad Kenya had ordered rustled beneath their feet. He was reminded of the mare he had ridden into the ground and then had slain, but his thoughts still dwelled in part on his neighbours. What would they get up to? He no longer opened his eyes as he had occasionally done hours ago, when he had sensed he was alone in his room. He felt himself being lifted up. Hands took him by the head and feet. Not gently, but with reluctance and full of disgust. It was an effort to keep himself rigid and he would rather have slumped, but it would be only for a few more moments. Steel himself, and then afterwards he would no longer be able to ruin the course of events. He was thrown, rather than laid, into the coffin. Skin and scab were scraped from his gangrenous thighs, causing them to drip blood and serum. He felt a seething pain and it was difficult to master his scream. He silently lamented that they had lain him naked on hard wood. Without a sheet. When there were so many in the linen chests. He listened, someone remarked that the wound stank. Such a foul calumny. A plank was hastily placed on the coffin as a lid. It turned out that the body lay crooked in its narrow confines and one shoulder jutted up above the edge of the casket. The board was placed on top, and someone used it for a seat. In this fashion Kebad Kenya's body was squeezed down. Settled in. Then they began driving nails into the wood. They must have been long and hard, this was obvious from the sound of their song, rising in pitch, and from the heaviness of the hammer blows. The neighbours had not scrimped here. Kebad Kenya counted two score nails. The wood creaked and groaned, splitting directly above his head, so that a splinter was driven into his scalp. There came silence and darkness, such as Kebad Kenya had never known. He began to feel afraid, wanted to cry out. But his voice failed him. It would also have been contrary to his innermost desires to emit a sound. Perhaps he was overcome by a brief sleep. Or had he fainted? At any rate, his lack of sensation was profound. He awoke to register a swaying motion performed by the casket and thus himself. It did nothing to ease his discomfort. Should this boat-like rocking continue for long, he would have to vomit. For the time being he tried to conquer his nausea. The days of fasting now proved to have been a useful preparation. He had given no forethought to the details of his experiences; but the course of events seemed nimbly to avoid the worst mishaps with no need of calculation or wisdom on his part. The sounds that penetrated the coffin permitted him the conclusion that he had been carried out, and was now being pushed on to a cart, with little care or ceremony. The horses set off at once. The neighbours seemed to be in a great hurry. They did not even shrink from picking up a gallop. The road was bumpy. Potholes and ridges followed one after the other. The servants had failed in their duty, but it was too late now to think of punishing them. No one would have heard the prostrate man had he raised his voice, for the wheels were rattling too loudly along the uneven road. It was hideous the way the unsecured coffin was tossed from side to side, jolting about erratically and crashing against the sides of the cart like a tree trunk. Kebad Kenya stretched out his hands as though he could have grasped the reins, but he reached into emptiness. His face buffeted against the nearby impediment. He already resembled a thing. He was screwed tightly into his narrow confines. His pains seemed not to have enough space beside him; they lay like a damp dew on the outside of the coffin. The road seemed as though it would never end. Whenever the horses slackened their pace the whip whistled across their rumps. The casket gave a jolt, tumbled, danced. The neighbours were in a great hurry.

Since all these events were bound by time and not eternity, the cart arrived at its destination. For a moment it had seemed to Kebad Kenya as if he were travelling the never-ending road to infinity. He tried to prepare a speech to explain or excuse his sin. Even though his words would first have been heard beyond the stars. Very late. It was possible too that no one would even understand what he was saying. That he had been alone. As if the infinite expanses were not more lonely. As if the ceaseless course of time had not savoured mankind's fate a thousandfold. What companions does the wind have? Nevertheless, Kebad Kenya could no longer retract his deceit — that he had died. And when a man is hated by death, then patience has to be found, or self-command, in order to await what must happen. After the cart had been brought to a halt — and the horses, there must have been four of them, gave a last snort — Kebad Kenya sensed no more than a few abrupt movements. He pictured to himself that he had been lowered somewhere. By ropes, he assumed. Perhaps they had made more elaborate arrangements, a foundation-pit with a ramp on one side. Wagons driving away, the crunch of horses' hooves on gravel. Men's footsteps above. Heavy stones, embedded in a swelling mass of lime, were placed over him. It grew quieter and quieter. The men's footsteps, still busy above, sounded muffled, coming to him as if from distant chambers. Gradually their sound became as slight as a whispering in the grass. After a while, when Kebad Kenya listened, all was still above. Possibly the wind swept through the branches of the undergrowth. It was of no consequence. An illusion. A nothingness. He wanted to ascertain within himself whether he had at last outwitted death. But he found it hard to fix his thoughts on this question. Not because it had become irrelevant to him. It had simply become unbelievably difficult to attain concepts by means of words. It seemed to Kebad Kenya that he needed a day, and even longer, to assign a single syllable to its corresponding image. Understandable, he was tired. The neighbours, he needed a whole year to think back to them and their menial business, he was that drowsy.

In the midst of this attenuated slowness he still perceived a thing or two. He had not lost his sense of touch. On the contrary, this sense appeared to become more subtle and to spin itself around him like a web of stuff more delicate than hair. His hearing seemed to have become clouded with deafness. Whether deafness in him or silence without, it hardly mattered. Even if it were imperative to establish this, the means were denied him because he could not move but only think, slowly, with remarkable slowness. His eyes likewise seemed to lapse into blindness. The darkness was not bound by the opening and closing of his lids. It seemed simpler to leave them permanently open — although it was fairly incomprehensible why he chose precisely this alternative. Whether the cause of the surrounding blackness was blindness within or darkness without, was a question that paralleled that of his hearing. Kebad Kenya would certainly have held himself for dead and as victor over his opponent, the masculine angel of death, had this spider's web of finest perceptions not been cast over him. He felt himself swell up. It did not unsettle him in the least. He expanded. It was contrary to reason. Gradually he filled the coffin right into its furthermost corners, and assumed the shape of a large, rectangular prism. He was afraid of bursting the grave, the coffin, the masonry. It was not a true fear, not even uneasiness; concepts like that were too concrete, anchored in ineluctable meanings; they had to be countermanded. Expectancy of a casual, provisional surprise. The monotonous, almost dreary consideration of a possibility extinguished before the coarse words could be summoned and revoked. The excess failed to manifest. Just as Kebad Kenya had gained more, but had lost it again. The spider's web in which he lay informed him that he would now decay, and defoliate. Defoliate, said the spider's web. And wither. Resemble a tree in winter. That bones were being referred to, his bones, which he had always possessed — he did not understand this properly. He was filled with sorrow that he would have to forgo his countenance. Slowly the certainty grew in him that his features were gone. There was no more controlling his appearance. He was like everyone. Had someone held a mirror before him — this trace of a thought was beyond him, but with the passing of the decades its impression made itself felt — he would no longer have recognised himself. Slowly it seeped into his consciousness that not only was his head alien to him, but his whole human form. The feeling of pain had completely slipped away. He felt himself rather commonplace. His sin — he thought about it only rarely — also seemed to have become but one element within some general order. And he had forgotten the speech he intended to make beyond the stars. Difficult to determine what it had been about. So much time seemed to have slipped by between the sin and its recognition, such wastes of solitude had opened up, that it was no longer possible to identify the sinner with the repentant. It was beyond all imagining why a judgement should ever come into being in this situation among the eternities, let alone a just judgement. The course of eternity would probably exhaust itself with tribunals. Thus keeping silence was the most sensible thing to do. Misunderstandings, should any arise, would then issue on their own.

The slower Kebad Kenya perceived, or understood, the faster time flowed. He was extremely astonished at finding himself very well rested after two centuries. He was also astonished to hear groaning and creaking above. His thoughts took on an alacrity quite contrary to his behaviour up until then. He felt, in as far as the importance of every feeling did not pale before this frenzied flight for which he now prepared himself, that his breast was being staved in. That after a few centuries, he had died. But he did not see the countenance of the male angel. At the same time his death was the start of an ever-increasing acceleration. Or the continuation of his flight. He could not understand whence came the power for this, for the silent envoy was not at hand; but it was present, incomprehensibly accumulated, ready to burst open the grave. The masonry was torn apart, probably by the power of his adversary, who did not reveal himself. Kebad

Hans Henny Jahnn

Kenya whispered the name: Malach Ha-Mavis.[1]

Kebad Kenya was raised up, turned to ashes, scattered, collected himself together again. He looked down as if from a great height. Somewhere a grave had been desecrated. Stones had been heaped up like rubble. Bones scattered about. Oak boards split apart. People were standing, looking inquisitively into a crater-like hole. A consuming gaze observed them from above. Yet Kebad Kenya was also below. Was lying with his limbs torn asunder. Not merely quartered. His heart ended up beneath the sole of a boot, but trampled on by one who did not care, or played the brute. The thighs, already dismembered many times over, were hacked apart with shovels. Kebad Kenya dived into the cluster of people in a wild frenzy, unable to tell whether he was driven by rage or madness. But they were left untouched. A few shivered, as if they were cold. It was incomprehensible how Kebad Kenya could lie there, mutilated, and simultaneously propel himself in flight. It was just a momentous urge, to stretch out, to be, and compress himself again into a narrow form. But his countenance, he recalled, had been dispersed to the winds. Even though he believed he saw it beneath him, beside him, all and everywhere, it disappeared as soon as he tried to assume any of its features. It was as if, over a great distance, he saw the portrait of the man which had been removed from a wall in his house and which was supposed to represent the person who had fathered him. He hurried up to it at once, studied the painted features. The portrait was displayed in a place he had never seen before. It had darkened. It hung in the proximity of numerous paintings that were darker still. He

1. Yiddish name for the Angel of Death. [Trans.]

recognised himself in the representation, even though it must have been older than he. But he also encountered himself emerging from another portrait, a century older. Had he the leisure to wonder at it, his astonishment would have been boundless. The older of the brown countenances raised him up, placed him on a tower. There were jackdaws flying about the tower. But they were slow in comparison with his flight. Stony heads stared at him. One resembled him, it was him, petrified, and yet reduced to dust by the ages. Scarcely had he registered this, this self, than he was already being driven on again. He fled, away from the sun, into the night. He recognised himself, trotting heavily, four-footed, furnished with hoofs, on a sandy steppe. Then immediately he sprouted wings, rose up, whinnying. He opened aged nostrils in the night air. Some power or other chased him back across a thousand miles, as if he had a place called home. A servant had pulled coins from under a dying man's pillow. A servant slept in a house standing on the spot where the old one, laid waste a century before, once stood. Kebad Kenya threw himself on the sleeping servant, and in the same moment recognised him as his own self. What figure could be more recognisable than this? What were portraits and stones compared with this sweet, living flesh? Had he judged himself in vain? Had the petitions he had made for his own case been turned down? Had someone tried — solely so as to make him grasp the vanity of his efforts — to instil within him something of the ever-present youthfulness of creation so that he would not flag and leave off committing his sin out of fatigue? He had not been heard. He was to persist in his vice, as he had for millennia. He arose from his bed. His mare was dead. The neighbours had slain her, but were there not others in his neighbours' stables? He rubbed his eyes. What could be easier than to force his way in? If he didn't know the layout of their houses, he could reconnoitre. He set off. The night was in his favour. It was an easy matter to break down a door. A horse led out. Not a sexless creature, a mare. Swing himself up on to her back, fly off like the wind. Ride her into the ground. Leave her on the wayside, to drag herself wearily home. Steal another. His thighs were no longer sensitive, the old wounds had healed. Gradually he recognised the landscape once more. The forests had been cleared. New roads had been cut into the sides of the hills. The smell rising from the soil was acrid and unhealthy. But the wind that blew across was the wind of old. The brooks still ran their courses. The pebbles in them fresh and hard. Reeds murmured by the ponds. The stars, he recognised them once again. It was his land, ravaged by the rapacity of his neighbours. This discovery hardly touched him. Sweat and breath of horse assailed his skin. The unchangeable animal smell which made him reel. The darkness of the earth, the darkness of the inner flesh. Once more the rapturous pain of being amidst these darknesses. Reality rolled off him like water from an oily surface; but he remained. A morning arrived. Days came. Nights came. He saw his neighbours multiply. Increase a thousandfold. They harried one another, got in each other's way. Kebad Kenya, with sweet flesh, laughed scornfully. He stole their horses by night, to regain his land, to commit his sin. The neighbours informed the police. Men in uniform arrived. He was truly amazed that they imagined they could catch him. They did not catch him. The neighbours cried to heaven that their mares were being ravaged.

Sassanid King

Not far from Mount Bistun and the City of Sarpul, close to the river
Karasu, which was already described by Tacitus, is a monument hewn in
the cliffs which the Arabs considered one of the Wonders of the World;
the poet Amru bin Bahr al-Jahiz wrote of it thus in his *Book of Countries*:
"There we find the depiction of a horse, and it must be the most beautiful
image that exists. It is said to be the portrait of Khisra's steed named
Shabdiz. Mounted on it is Khisra, carved in stone. And the portrait of his
wife Shirin is located in the upper storey of this grotto."

In the year 1228 the encyclopædist Yaqut of Hama finished his great
book of names and began his reminiscences of the last of the mighty
Sassanid dynasty with the name of the king's favourite mare. He describes
the location of the monument, this vital (albeit stone) testimony, without
which one would glean naught of the story of this happiest of men except
as if through a veil. It may be discerned in the outward lineaments of his
last year of rule, which were filled by the wars against Heraclius, that
imprudent Christian who was destined to dash the final chalice of
fulfilment from the hand of the fortunate one, and to grind down this

magnificent edifice of unprecedented favouritism granted by the hand of fate.

The idea of a war over the Holy Cross of Jesus, the dark omens of floods and disease, the blazing portents of comets that announced the influence of the Prophet Mohammed in the lands outside of Arabia, would otherwise have obliterated the life of this individual.

We foolish men want to hang doggedly to the notion that it is the struggles, victories and defeats of great maxims that move our hearts and prompt its decisions. Lies. The most audacious and spiritual abstraction is but a bag of bones without the living flesh of the individual. The gluttony of an earthly child contains more reason than the pious charity of a dried-up old woman who no longer has the courage for even the tiniest of her desires.

This place that the Muslims have often described is characterised by a marble mountain from which gush copious springs. Since time immemorial it was a sacred place for the Iranis, who believed they must worship the goddess Anahit[1] beside the clear waters spawned by stone.

Two grottoes have been cleaved from the dense limestone rocks; the smaller, which had been hollowed out on the orders of Shapur III, borders directly on a larger one, the monument to Shabdiz and her master.

Encyclopædia 1228: "Shabdiz is a site located between Hulwan and Qarmisin at the foot of Mount Bistun, and is named after a horse that

1. Anahit was the goddess of fertility and healing, wisdom and water in Armenian mythology. [Trans.]

belonged to Khosrau."

Mis'ar b. al-Muhalhil tells us that: "the image of Shabdiz is at a distance of one parasang from the city of Qarmisin. It shows a man mounted on a horse of stone, clad in invincible armour made of iron. Whose coat of mail is visible. And with studs to the coat of mail. There can be no doubt, all who see it thinks it moves. This image is that of Parviz[2] on his steed, Shabdiz. There is no image that is its like on all the Earth. There are a number of images in the grotto that contains this image. Images of men and women, on foot and on horseback. Before the grotto is a man who looks like someone with a cap on his head. And he is girded about the waist. In his hand is a hoe, as if he were about to dig the soil. Water wells up from under his feet."

Ahmad b. Mohammed al-Hamadhani says: "Among the wonders of Qarmisin — and it is verily one of the wonders of the world — is the image of Shabdiz. It is located in a village called Khatan. And the sculptor was Qattus b. Sinimmar. Sinimmar is the one who built the Khaournaq palace in Kufa. The reason for the depiction of the steed in this village was that she was the largest and most pure of animals. Whose nature was the most apparent. And had the greatest endurance at the gallop. The king of the Indians had made a present of her to Parviz. She neither staled nor defecated as long as she was harnessed and saddled. Nor did she snort or champ. The measure of her hoof was six spans. Then it came to pass that Shabdiz fell ill. And her ills worsened. Parviz learned of this and spoke:

2. I.e. Khosrau Parviz. [Trans.]

'Verily, if anyone announces the death of my horse I shall kill him!' So when Shabdiz died, her equerry feared that the king would ask him and that he would have no choice but to divulge her death, and that the king would kill him. So he went to the king's singer, Pahlbadh, whose accomplishment in song and lute knew no comparison, before or since. It is said that Parviz had three special things that none had had before: his steed Shabdiz, his slave girl Shirin, and his singer Pahlbadh. The equerry spoke: 'Know that Shabdiz has perished and died. You are aware of the threat the king has made to anyone who announces her death. Therefore devise a ploy, and so and so much will be yours.' The other man agreed to the ploy. And during an audience with the king he sang him a song in which the story was concealed, until the king understood and cried out: 'Woe betide you, Shabdiz is dead!' The singer replied: 'The king is saying this!' To which the king replied: 'Ah, agreed, you are saved and have saved another.' And he grieved deeply for his horse. And he commanded Qattus b. Sinimmar to portray her. He depicted her in the loveliest and most perfect manner, so that there was scarcely any difference between the two except in the pulsating of the vital spark in their bodies. The king came to see and shed tears as he looked upon her. And he said: 'The depiction foreshadows in great measure our own death. It reminds us of what a sad state we shall reach. If in this moment there is one thing among the things of the world that points to the things of that other world, then lo, it is this that causes us to recognise the death of our bodies and the destruction of our physical raiments and the disappearance of our human form and the obliteration of our every trace through putrefaction, which none may escape. And simultaneously to recognise the impression left by that which cannot possibly survive from the beauty of our form. The contemplation of this representation has served to remind us of what we shall become, and we picture to ourselves how others will come after us and linger here, so it is as if we were part of them and here with them.'"

Ahmad b. Mohammed al-Hamadhani states further: "Among the wonders of this form is that no form exists like this one. And no one having an astute mind and fine judgement can have lingered before it since the day it was made without harbouring doubts about its form and marvelling at it. Yes, I have heard many swear as much and almost utter on oath that it cannot be the work of a mortal, and that Allah the all-mighty is the keeper of a secret that he will one day reveal."

If this representation is the work of human hands, then this sculptor has talent such as no other master possesses. For what is more wondrous or beautiful, or fraught with more obstacles, than making the rock as malleable as he did; and that it became black where it had to be black, and red where it had to be red; and likewise with the other colours. And it is clear to me that the colours were treated in a particular manner.

Spreading all about the holy mountain with its holy springs were the hunting grounds of the king. He sought to dissolve his grief at the death of his mare in a tidal wave of desire in which he allowed his heavy body to wallow in the extensive gardens.

He wept with one eye only. His lecherous lips drank fermented wine, mulled with nutmeg, honey, cloves, Chinese ginger and cinnamon. His teeth pick fleshy crusts from dessicated roasts. He sees the stone horse, and riding on it the stone king, his own self. He sucks the vital juices and grease from his fingers. Half drunk he sinks down on a woman's breasts. He weeps, he drinks, naked thighs open up to him.

The beginning of his rule had been accompanied by violent disruptions. Bahrām Chobin, last of the great Mihrans, had brought the Sassanid Empire to the verge of destruction. Crazed with power. Dominion, oppression, wading through blood. Khosrau's father, Hormizd, was blinded and then put to the spear; he himself, the son, the young Grand King, was compelled to flee to Byzantium to the Emperor Maurikios. But Bahrām's fortune came to an end. A simple murder removed him. Iron and flesh.

Maurikios, Emperor of the Byzantines, conferred upon Khosrau, the youngster who had travelled through Asia Minor...

His father put to the spear. Iron and flesh.

You trembled. Were afraid. You wept. Rode horses. Thighs sore. Along stony roads. And assistants were sent to look.

Conferred upon him the right to rule.

Called to fortune. Grown like a bull in the bizarre orgies of Byzantium. The hour came. The emperor, the benefactor, the Byzantine, the man praying under the gigantic dome of Santa Sophia, fell, as if senseless. The incompetent Phocas — son of a she-dog, a woman, mated by seventy men — this Phocas staged a successful rebellion. And celebrated his victory by having Maurikios and his entire family slaughtered. Like cattle. And disembowelled. For the dogs. Son of a she-dog.

Perhaps there had been a moment after this bloody event in which Khosrau had felt called to wage war against Phocas to avenge his benefactor. Was it not the bloody pain and anger at the loss of his friend that led him to send the first legions out against Eastern Rome?

Phocas, son of a she-dog, of seventy fathers, eliminated Narses, the administrator of the eastern provinces, a torch, a genius of a general who blazed in the face of Persia.

Iran now knows no peace. The first generals sent out by the Grand King were able to report unblemished victories. This was in the year of our Lord 604.

In the following year of our Lord, 605, the Sassanid cavalry swept through the eastern provinces of the Byzantine Empire in wild forays. The king's desire for riches flared up in his "gateways", his cities. Thirsting like no other for jewels, he ordered raids on the empire of his erstwhile benefactor and the son of a she-dog who currently insulted him.

Perhaps Maurikios had been forgotten. The memory of how he had died dispelled in the face of new possibilities of immeasurable happiness, which Khosrau wished to concentrate on one person, himself. With fanatical eloquence he conveyed to his generals that they were only to have one desire, one duty, one goal: victory. Victory in order to capture booty. Booty captured so as to render to the king immeasurable riches and contentment. For twenty whole years he drove his armies through Mesopotamia, Syria, Palestine, Phoenicia, Armenia, Cappadocia, Galatia and Paphlagonia. Gold, precious gems, mechanical marvels, statues and women flowed to him in streams. He took all that had been grown or shaped to be beautiful, never tiring in his pleasure. He regarded the first great defeat of his troops as a deliberate personal insult on the part of his general. He believed he was free of fate. For certain reasons. (Holy Cross, Labartu.)

I have come this far. Seven times saved from death. On horseback through Asia Minor. Thighs and anus raw. I stayed alive. In those days I was not yet fat. My belly was but a boy's. Maurikios said: "Lovely boy."

This Saens — defeated general. He had fallen ill. He died during the retreat.

He is to be put in salt so that his corpse does not rot!

The dead man was made to appear before the king, to justify himself. He remained silent, salty, slightly desiccated, remained silent, obdurate, did not answer his king. So judgement was passed on him to be flayed. He was wrested from putrefaction so as to be torn and mangled before Khosrau's eyes. The king felt insulted. That was the end of the dead man, after the living man had been beaten in the year of our lord 626 by Theodorus, brother of Emperor Heraclius.

The eyes of the king.

The senses of the king.

The fortune of the king.

Long live the king.

Armoured cavalry, instrument of war, people, horses, leather, metal. They sang of women. They were chased from country to country. They sang of catamites. They were chased from province to province. Mesopotamia, Syria, Palestine, Phoenicia, Armenia, Cappadocia, Galatia and Paphlagonia. They were the moment that no one held on to, save the women they made pregnant. The king was the rock. He kept the women whom he chanced to like.

They plundered, murdered. Wanton rape, profligacy, the spectacle of human dwellings and forests burning each night. The lust of the one, the lust of the other.

In the year of our Lord 614 Shahrbaraz Farrukhan, the great general of Khosrau (insatiable in his fortune), entered Jerusalem. The Christians had buried the Holy Cross, the greatest sacred object in the Holy City, lest it fall into the hands of the infidels. There is no silence that cannot be broken (except the final silence that spells death). The conquerors took the pious body of Patriarch Zacharias and tortured him. There was no end and no measure to the pains they inflicted on him, no device they shunned before he began to speak. The tradition of the ten thousand murders was exercised on his living frame (which they knew how to keep alive; and so that he did not faint, smelling salts. People do not faint if one beats the ribs above the heart with wooden mallets), who now, learning from the pains (ninety thousand transported into slavery), came up with a more convenient piety and divulged the location where the symbol was buried, the wood that is, the executioner's tool, Roman gallows, the block, axe, wheel, slaughterhouse (O Lamb — of God — innocent). Shahrbaraz wanted to see his master smile; he carried off the cross (ninety thousand transported into slavery).

Inscrutable, this man shattered the wood, gave a piece of it to his Christian Minister of Finance, Yazdin, and locked up the instrument of martyrdom with a great show of pomp and reverence (the inscrutable Parviz) for the tenets of an alien faith, in the new treasury and state prison at Ctesiphon, the "House of Darkness", believing that the magical powers of the Unknown would from now on be at his behest, would enhance his fortune. Like Labartu, the goddess of pestilence who was held captive next to the Holy Cross.

She was old, very old and mightier than the Cross. She had come from Babylon or Nineveh. Lion-headed with pointed ass's ears. Woman, breasts of woman, woman who had borne and suckled a pig and a wolf. Snakes in her hands; growing from her sex an eagle's legs, with which she squats on an ass; her leman with her, who is encamped in a ship that bears these lovers along the rivers; that sows pus with its fertility.

The king heaved a sigh when one of his generals found and dragged up this savage power of destruction. He feared disease; he had grown fat. He had stood grinning before the stone building, then hurried off again, had adorned himself like a fabled beast. Gaudy. Silk of seven hues. Five basic colours: red, green, blue, yellow, white, plus the highlights, the bow of Abraxas, the sun and the starry sky, gold and black. Plus the attribute, the precious gems. He had whipped up the court to an unheard-of celebration. Processions, parades before the gaze of the dread demon. Labartu, plague goddess, ass's lover. Servants and generals must copulate with she-asses. To make her smile. In the dust before her. Most debasing lust. I command it! Your health demands it, my fat belly. No disorder may arise. What I eat in the evening must pass out of me again by the morning, or else the sun will brew ass seeds from it for Labartu.

Then the stone was sunk into the grottoes of the prison.

The king was immune to disease, to the challenges of a mutable body.

He proclaimed health upon his lands. They did not grumble. Not even the lovers of the ass. Health. No fever. No smells in the still bays of the waters.

He assumed the certainty of eternal youth and eternal strength.

He selected three thousand women who would accommodate the immeasurable abundance of his loins. There were eight thousand girls for the momentary stilling of his sensuous manifestations. He resembled a luxuriant golden meadow that filled the heavens with the perfumed vapours of their couplings.

He grew to become the owner of twelve incomparable treasures, attributes and requisites of power.

1. The Palace of Ctesiphon.

2. Khosrau's throne. A mechanical clock, a work of unsurpassable sensitivity and calculation.

3. The crown decorated with the three largest jewels in the world, which Alexander's stallion Bucephalus had pawed from the sands of India; and of which the Arabs were later to say: large as ostrich eggs. Mysterious inscriptions in Greek characters that were the key to beneficial powers, raised the value of these stones beyond all material measure.

4. A chess set with figures carved from emeralds and rubies.

5. Gold as malleable as wax.

6. The Ganj-i-badh-award,[3] which constituted the entire fortune of Alexandria, laden during the siege of the city by the Greeks on to ships and then captured; and the kanz al-thaur, a collection of treasures from

3. "The Treasure brought by the Wind". [Trans.]

45

fabled times, turned up while ploughing the soil.

7. His mistress, Shirin, the Garden of Beauty.

8. His mare Shabdiz.

9. The singers Sardjis and Pahlbadh.

10. A white elephant.

11. The Holy Flag of Iran, the leather apron of the legendary smith Kawa.

12. The page and culinarist Khosharzu.

But his true love was Shirin. She was as fine as eleven thousand. Garden of Beauty. Gushing Spring.

And Shabdiz, the mare.

And he built her a monument, the Taqi Bustan, when Shabdiz died. The death of his charger marked the end of his confidence and occasioned sorrowful words. As if through tears he looked once again at his fortune before the body of the mare. He was transported by the words of his injured soul. A cave hewn into the marble. Inside one can see depicted the many stages of the life that was Khosrau's and that had made him rich; and the gods that had chosen him to show with uncommon measure the impact of a human life. In the rear of the grotto, on its lower floor, as it were, the king, riding on the nocturnal mare. He is wrapped, war-like, in the scent of the beast. Her sweat does not trouble this sensitive man — who had experienced such difficulties with the smell of business scrolls that he obliterated it with saffron and rose water — who felt secure because the contact, warm, the unspeakable rises up through his thighs, from the hair of the animal on which he balances, not gird with chainmail.

"The sapphire pen of night has cleansed blue your white most blue."

Shirin is not portrayed. The three thousand concubines are depicted on the monument. Shirin was kept hidden from the mason. The existence of the king seeped through his mask and collected like water in a basin. Basins of silver, of granite, of bronze, of lapis lazuli, of pewter, of basalt, of copper, of diorite, of gold, of clay. Shards and dents are their fate.

The passion of the sculptor Farhad had made him uncertain. The story was told later, encumbered with circumlocutions. Shirin took delight in Farhad. She did not abandon him to Khosrau's rage when she became aware of his intentions. She ingratiated him to the king, invented virtues for him, gave the Grand Prince to understand that he was his equal as a man. She did not forget to stress his magnanimity, his readiness for liberty, his selflessness, his willingness for sacrifice. If Khosrau did not wish to seem small, to run the danger of being called a tyrant whom not even Shirin loved, he had to acknowledge the qualities that were credited to the other. He would yield his lover's bed to him on one condition. In his scepticism he demanded a test. The royal sceptic demanded a hard test. They ride into the mountains. The three of them. The woman, the two men, selfless, magnanimous, ready for sacrifice, free, slaves only to themselves, the king and the sculptor. Did Khosrau realise from the briny flavour of his spittle that he had taken on the smaller role, that the task he had thought up would not only test the lover, but above all himself?

They made a pact before a mountain. The king smiling, not utterly humiliated, not completely transformed into a buffoon, still king with rights to his own wife; the opponent radiant, because he had remained alive, because the prize depended on his efforts and abilities.

Farhad has to dig a tunnel through the mountain. If he succeeds, the king must share the marital bed.

He starts to carve the mountain. Khosrau, who has no eye for this, who cannot judge the force required, is seized by restlessness. A report reaches him: Farhad has covered half the distance through the rock. The king is no hero. He can gather treasures, amass money. He is like a bull in his siring. No hero. His generals are heroes. The sculptor is one. The man on the throne enjoys pleasure. He is fat. Farhad slender and wiry. Khosrau feels his heart. He looks round for familiar faces. He is abandoned. King, King. Maurikios had caressed his nipples when he was still without power.

He believed in the other's love for Shirin, but not in his own. He sends a messenger to Farhad. The messenger tells him: "Shirin is dead." It is a lie from the mouth of the king, Farhad hurls himself from the cliff. The king's peace of mind is dashed. He begins to treat his own love for Shirin like a dogma. Dangers gather. He does not know their names. It is announced that the plague has penetrated the borders of his realm. He has extra guards placed on Labartu in the treasury. But comets chase across the skies. He knows neither their names nor their paths.

Shabdiz is dead. She defecated in death. The generals win. Khosrau's victory is minor, unheroic. He hunts. Deer, boar, ducks. The women watch on. Even animals have blood in them. But they do not scream. Silent pain. So they have no feeling. He believes this. Because he can scream. Their entrails are not Khosrau's entrails. He believes this. Because he has yet to see himself from inside. He will learn. Their siring is not his siring. Their progeny is not his progeny. He will learn. Martyred game. Martyred king.

Blossoms bloom. Two pillars blossom. Two marble rocks blossom. They blossom to the rhythm of the acanthus. They smell rosy white like spirals. A breeze lies in the leaves and spreads like a fan. Buds form when one thinks of fans. When a bud forms, it becomes three. Wherever three forms, the lotus blossom floats, blue, pale, seven times folded. When it sheds its petals sevenfold, the labyrinth of stamens, saffron, seed, bud and fruit bursts forth. Time and eternity. Marble pillars blossom to the left and right of the grotto. Acanthus leaves form themselves like a fan. The spiral is a curve of the third or fourth order, the mathematicians tell us. The trunk is round and towers up to the skies.

Behind the pillars, in the depths of the cave, Khosrau hunts on his charger, in a boat, encircled by elephants. Three thousand women surround him, admiring his shallow heroism, Shirin is not among them. She is in childbed. She has given birth to a boy. Poor boy! "Khosrau loves you." The king writes his distinguishing mark. He ranks the women according to the pleasure they give him. He does not tell them. He has it woven in silk. He wants to live free of strife.

Small, frothy clouds of happiness like waves. Pleasure with eyes closed. Nothing more. Not a word. Breasts and thighs. Not a word. Little golden clouds of happiness against a black background, like night and velvety skin. By adding three small spheres to this, the symbol of the chintamani, he wants to remember more deeply, not merely fumble.

A person, a prophet, Mohammed had preached. In Arabia. Word came of this. Khosrau's eyes became impotent, raging, impotent. Maurikios had caressed, young, his nipples. Dead. Heraclius the name of the present emperor. The generals win; taxes crush the land. Four-quartered lotus blossom, four petals like hearts. Nocturnal lotus blossoms, each as beautiful as the other. They all have a depression at the centre of the calyx. Scattered over his robes, does it signify the king? — nocturnal lotus blossoms, closed, half-open, ripe, fleshy like a draught of syrup.

And so that the nights grow darker and long, one braids a hem of lotus blossoms, of buds, of lotus blossom buds, split thrice, split five, split seven times. Buds two in number. They are the breasts, lovelier than the sex.

Across the mountains a duet, a man and a boy. Shepherds by their flocks. Endlessly sad. Sadness of the world.

Tears, tears, tears, tears.

And the night can grow denser, the sweetness denser. Interweaves blossoms and buds, thick as a thicket. Handle-shaped buds. Curving till opening. A game as if on the squares of a chessboard. Khosrau does not need a divan. Khosrau sleeps between the thighs of the women. They harp his dreams to him.

The woman resting there, the woman resting there, the mother of Ninazu.

The name of his dream is Shirin. Shirin has given birth to a son. He is not the oldest son. He is the son that the king loves. Because he loves Shirin. It is not Farhad's son. Farhad is dead. Shabdiz is dead. Maurikios is dead. Phocas, son of a she-dog, son of seventy fathers, murdered, dead.

The gold coins mounted up in his treasuries. Round coins. Dead fortune. Fortune. He did not realise it was dead. He had it woven into silk. Happy hours. Dead happy hours. He did not know. The women playing violins

knew it. They were coins. They ran through his hand; then they rested like
the gold in his treasury. And if they were blessed they became pregnant,
likewise became round. Coins. Words could be written in the roundness of
the disc, words by which Khosrau could distinguish them, and recall the
occasion on which he had seen them for the first or last time. Peacocks,
boars' heads, flowers, stones, herons, rams, suns, stars, clouds.

There were any number of them, for them he wrote in their presence,
with effort, in a language of wordless magnificence, from the memories of
his passion. His mind sought confirmation, rained down bolts of ardent
creative fervour on to matter. He further corroborated comparisons with
the animals in the field and the animals of dreams through the sweat of his
quest. He brought both the real and the unreal to blaze up in cataracts of
fiery colours. Topics malleable as gold. Elaborated laws for the growth of
plants, from within, like a god inside the seed-pod. Intertwined into
lozenges, they were compelled to form ornaments, and then congeal into
their foliage and latticework and frame the animals of the fields, the
winged sheep, the clawed horses, the proud and ruffled birds. His plans
were carried out by dextrous weavers. The idea rampaged across the stone.
The stone began to bud, to blossom.

The time had come when he must account for his actions. His generals
were conquered in open battle. The sons of the soldiers, adult, fought
against soldiers. For they were their mothers' sons.

The provinces tired of growing lean for the king's happiness.

Ignorant of warfare, he has to flee from Ganzak before Heraclius's
army; aghast, he destroys his country; torches it; ravages the fields; drags

off the populace. In his horror at the tragedy, he thinks only of the most indispensable treasures, of the attributes and requisites of power, of the money, of the sacred fire, of the charcoal oracle of Ganzak.

His wickedness worsened. Heraclius's troops, Christians who had admired and then destroyed the capital of the Medes, marched from their Albanian winter quarters out on to the Babylonian plain.

Khosrau trembles. He is no hero. Secretly, by night, accompanied by just the few closest to his heart, he steals from the palace, Dastagerd, that cannot be captured in battle. Even the heavy walls of Ctesiphon do not seem safe to him. Off to Seleucia. Once I fled through Asia Minor. Am fleeing again.

The Christian marches into Dastagerd without a struggle, writes a letter to the senate in Byzantium, which is studiously read from the pulpit of Hagia Sophia by diligent and patriotic servants of a faith that is at enmity with nations (O Lamb — of God — innocent), in which the astonishment, the improbability, the great whore of constancy is announced in the ripe sentence: "Who would have thought it!"

Heraclius was forced to turn back before Ctesiphon. Khosrau's elephant cavalry pushed its way forward along the banks of a canal. Grey ghostlike stamping. The shadows of a joyous life.

For his part, the king wrote a justification of his life. In it he declared himself to be the kind of person who may be condemned under specific constellations. Explained he was forced to flee to Seleucia; only far from danger would he be able to use his creative mind. From the outermost limits of his realm he had resolved to do what would save them, act wisely.

Trampling the Roman legions under the soles of the advancing elephants. (20,000 feet. A moving wall 100 feet deep and 3000 feet wide.) His calculations became the will of his generals. He once again turned the fate of his land to the good, having previously been taken by surprise, rather than the arts of an enemy general. Even so he claimed, what no one in his day could judge, that he was a good administrator, and an even better merchant. He balanced his accounts in figures.

At the end of my 13th year, after a year at war with the Emperor Phocas (son of a she-dog with seventy fathers), I had coins minted. After deductions for all the wages and other expenses, the sum of 400,000 bags of minted coin remained in the treasury.

At the end of my 30th year I again had coins minted. After deductions for all the wages and other expenses, the sum of 800,000 bags of minted coin remained in the treasury, the equivalent of 1,600 million mithqals.

Up until my 38th year this fortune grew unceasingly. Only once, when I was 18, did my fortune slump to 420 million mithqals, after the deduction of all expenses and allowances.

He realised that despite the victory of his herd of elephants he would have to abdicate. Fled to Seleucia. There must have been many among the nobility who could not forgive him for this. And he decided to abdicate from the throne. He abdicated in favour of his son whom he loved the most, who was not the oldest of his sons, in favour of the son of Shirin, who was only, the people said, his mistress.

However, this wish was taken as an even greater insult than his flight. Voluntary abdication was not to be countenanced. The children born earlier felt cheated. Unloved. Their mothers affronted. Sheroe, an older son (older than Shirin's boy), became spokesman for all who were neglected. He dictated the terms of abdication. His hatred spawned a trial for his own father and the beloved scion (loved by Khosrau, hated by Sheroe) of the fortunate one (Parviz). He, Sheroe, full of hatred, the new king, for whose sake Khosrau had not stepped down, issued a warrant for the two who loved each other, father and son. During the trial, conducted in the name of the people, the quondam king produced the careful accounts from his business scrolls (once sprinkled with rose water, dusted with saffron on account of the annoying smell) and finished his long speech in his defence by claiming he had governed his country well. (The overall balance was divulged.)

He was incarcerated (in the name of the people) in the House of Darkness at Ctesiphon, forced to inhale the breath from the mouth of Labartu (ass's lover). The symbol of eternally tormenting justice, cross, spider web, sign of the universe in the spatial, in the temporal, in the fourth dimension (positive, negative, rational, irrational, O Lamb — of — God — innocent), his extradition was negotiated in preliminary peace talks (Heraclius — Sheroe), the wood oppressed him with visions of those who had been nailed to it, who died on it (100,000. 1,000,000. Spartacus's uprising. Everyone they took prisoner was crucified).

For several days Sheroe pondered a plan, revenge, an act of hatred, the uninhibited course of a justice (in the name of the people). The fever had already begun to gain power over the ci-devant king Khosrau Parviz (the inscrutable, fortunate one). Then he (Sheroe, the new king, successor to

Khosrau) pronounced him guilty, which, as is well known, is an easier verdict than innocent, for it is brief, compared to the three-syllable word. And executioners appeared, people skilled in their craft, with certain instructions. They set up a butcher's block close by, before the eyes of the former king now clapped in irons, and placed upon it, alive, naked, bound, as was meet, the son of Shirin, likewise former king, usurper, as they said, and criminal; and began to carve him up before his father's eyes, beginning with the belly, they eviscerated him, cut out the dying son's heart, castrated him, removed his brain, his tongue, his lungs, his kidneys, and blinded him (O Lamb — of God — innocent). With a bestial, infernal gesture, Labartu's fever burst from Khosrau's veins as festering ulcers. Tormented game! Seven-petalled lotus blossom. Grotto of Paradise. Blossoming pillars. Spirals of the acanthus.

The king never learnt of Shirin's fate, whore in strangers' beds, for his ears refused to register sound. A few hours after his favourite son was slaughtered he was put to the spear. Like his father. And began to putrefy like his son, like Farhad, as Shabdiz had, first of all. As Shirin would do some day.

Sheroe was poisoned or died of the plague.

General Shahrbaraz, also king, for four weeks regent, then murdered.

Boran, Khosrau's daughter, regent, died.

Ardashir III, a child, the flood carried him away.

The Catholic Church celebrated the feast of Exaltatio Sanctae Crusis (O Lamb — of God — innocently slain on the shaft of the cross).

The soul of man has eternal life. The soul of the animal rots like the

body of the animal. And can be eaten like the body of the animal.
Your thighs are soft like the nostrils of a mule.
The yellow of saffron plays about your breasts.
The sapphire pen of night has cleansed blue your white most blue.
I'd be made of stone if I did not know your hidden behests.

A Master Selects his Servant

Manshard has quit my service. I had been feeling fractious and spoke sharply to him, unfairly. He answered at once with uncustomary vehemence, unthinking I felt. He almost screamed, saying he was sick of being used by me, of nursing my none-too-pleasant idiosyncrasies in return for a pittance. I am not aware of ever having requested anything untoward from him, of abusing his service. The claim that I pay him a pittance seems to be repudiated by the fact that in the same breath, he told me he was going to open a coffee shop and had saved up enough to be able to do so.

A feeling of unhappiness. We have spent many a year together. Probably they were a disappointment to him; I think he got bored because I hated change. His face gradually grew empty, hard to understand, alien. Admittedly it sometimes filled again when I told him he had to take me into town in the car, even when it was late in the evening. He was fanatical about driving me around, often asking me on a Sunday to choose some destination or other, as far away as possible, in a charming area. He also urged me to go on nocturnal adventures. And now this reproach that I often had not given him time off on Sundays and had kept him from his sleep.

So now he wants to open a coffee shop. That was probably his aim all along. And now is the moment. Service for him was but a step in that direction, to that goal. It is only I who am beset by a feeling of unease, of uncertainty, fear even, because I no longer know what kind of person I will have about me in the future.

I must curb my dismay, that goes without saying. I have inserted an advertisement in a number of newspapers. I composed a very exacting text for the purpose. And now these others have come to see me. People I do not know, have never seen before. I tried to appraise them, learn something about them. There were fewer than I had expected. A round dozen, no more — as if the position of a personal valet was no longer *au courant.*

They had to converse with me. Also to shave me so that I received a reliable impression of their skill, of the lightness of their touch. This allowed me to breathe in their odour, to discover whether it was pleasant, indifferent or repugnant. I studied their hands, their face, how much grace I could find in them. I had them take me out on a test drive to town and back. For each I rendered account in writing; in which I listed their particular qualities in terms of human education and appearance — in so far as these things affected me or were apparent to me. Finally I asked them their ages, had them show references, talk about their past.

Most were from the catering trade, had worked as waiters; others had learned the barber's trade; some of them were employed aboard ship.

Little emerged during these discussions that excited or attracted. Mundane lives and trifling adventures were described, while their actual characters remained concealed. Each had a flattering image of himself and praised — albeit in modest tones — his irreproachable conduct. None of them seemed to have any sense of conviction. No, I sensed scarcely a flicker of passion among them, or even of life. Be that as it may, a couple — the youngest of the applicants — seemed, if I had not totally mistaken their behaviour, willing to supplement their role as household companion with more personal duties. The extent of their willingness to serve lent them a kind of beautiful impudence, but not the appearance of being reliable. The large, powerful automobile threatened to rob these youngsters of their senses; at any rate their minds very quickly became blended with its speed. They could not know how much this displeased me. Nor did their suggestive smiles help.

I asked each to leave with the words that I had to think it over, and promised to reply in writing. It has proved difficult for me to decide, because not one of them even approximated my image of an amenable or agreeable person. Ultimately I had to admit to myself that even Manshard had only partly complied with my wishes regarding his nature and appearance; I had gradually grown accustomed to him. So my choice fell on an almost fifty-year-old man who shaved me with the deftness of a demigod, who, without my divulging my fears, drove the car with caution and only at moderate speeds, and without overlooking crossroads and paying attention to children at play — who sensed, it seemed, my anxious heart and was resolved to spare it.

His name is Wagner. The couple of references he showed me describe him as dependable, considerate and skilled. Some gentleman or other called him a born butler. He has only served in a few houses. In most cases his master's death had precipitated the change. I wrote him a letter with the conditions, and a rejection to all the others.

A few hours later a certain Herr von Uchri appeared, offering me his services. I should have explained to him at once that the position was taken, but I let him in and was soon in conversation with him. And now I am utterly confused, and quite unsettled, because I have taken him on as well.

I am attempting to clarify to myself how it came to this turn-about within me, to this surrender to chance. I have broken a fundamental rule. Why? Naturally I shall pay Wagner an appropriate sum by way of compensation. But why did I suddenly want the other in his stead? What marks him apart? At any rate, not a long career as a valet or butler.

Von Uchri — his full name is Ajax von Uchri — was not obliged to give a sample of his skills. I even know that he is unable to drive a car, and the first time he shaves me he will probably tear my face to shreds. He has only just turned twenty-four.

I was certainly not won over by his aristocratic descent, for as he himself admits, it is of the lowest rank. He did not speak respectfully of his family. He pointed to his facial features, which he analysed somewhat rudely. All of his ancestors are present in it, he remarked, this line of farmers, honourable merchants, learned clergymen, belly-splitting butchers, honest housewives, frivolous ladies and cavaliers. All frozen together in strife; dark secrets, ever-accruing vices, adventures, hours of dull indifference, lies, avarice, cunning, seemingly mature composure; screams, fears, tears, dreams of predation, staid conformity. Each has an inconsequential place on his skin. He was forced to repeat each squandered life in cold blood and sport this face, so he told me, that was the result of many translucent layers superimposed one on the other. He could smell the musty smell of stables — himself.

Does a normal person talk of such things?

After straying off like this his speech was once again sober and sensible. Without pausing for thought he told me that his father has been dead since he was seven. His mother was living out of wedlock with a farmer. An uncle without the patent of nobility had paid his school fees for ten whole years. This uncle had four daughters. Every day he would take the five of them to a little wood, through fields of cornflowers, across meadows, reciting the names of the flowers and birds and explaining their habits. He restricted himself to birds and flowers. When Ajax asked him once, in the presence of his daughters, whether he knew how rabbits mate, he was confined to his room for three days. The uncle felt that incarceration was meet for a scion of a noble lineage. He was never beaten. It was hinted to him that his father, who had probably had a small business in pepper and raisins, had been a merchant by appointment to a ducal house; the term "royal house" was avoided because it was not exactly a flourishing business. At any rate the father left him nothing — apart from a bat for some Mexican ball game, soaked in linseed oil.

At seventeen he ran away from his guardian, who wished to marry him to one of his daughters, because he had satisfied his curiosity with the older girl without a thought of marriage.

He became a waiter. His uncle never succeeded in finding him.

"After a few years Herr Dumenehould de Rochemont discovered me," he said, reaching into his coat pocket and handing me a letter. "Ajax is magnificent," I read, "whoever places their trust in him will gain more than he expects." Not another word, apart from a man's signature. Herr Dumenehould was a shipowner; he died a few months ago.

"He came across me in a bar. He heard someone calling my name. He checked with me that he had heard correctly. He told me that he had known my father. He knew that my father had not been a merchant to a duke. But that was no longer important because he was long since dead. Herr Dumenehould said he had once dandled me on his knees as a child. He had been to my father's office, which smelled of spices. The smells, the old wallpaper on the walls, the white painted window frames, the lofty entrance and the curls of grey stucco on the ceiling — it all returned with these words. He proposed that I move into his house as his butler, and I agreed. At that time I was receiving a paltry wage for a paltry job."

I listened on tenterhooks like a schoolboy to this man who wanted to be my servant. Perhaps taking a deep breath. I sensed a slight, almost imperceptible waft of perfume and simultaneously a slightly scorched smell as if from a tawny skin. I turned my face to the window in order to avert my attention — and as if this had been my first glimpse of the park that day, I saw in over-abundant clarity the grey of the clouds, the pale colour of the raindrops streaking down the windowpanes, the trickling waters of the heavens that darkened the green of the trees. Full of sudden resolve, I looked at von Uchri. His countenance flickered in strange commotion: full of promise, cheerful, roguish yet somehow strained. It was pleasing yet divided. Curious that for all its vivacity, the olive-brown skin — the clouds had coloured it so — had a slightly leaden cast — like a fragment from before history, a mask cast into life, melancholy as metal, relentless but sensual; a monument to an audacious pedigree. I was enchanted by this face because it contained such archaic forms, from which mouth and chin alone jutted out with feminine negritude. I studied it without reserve — as a welcome addition to the visible world.

My examination, this long gaze, may have offended decency; I cannot recall having ever studied a person with quite such penetration. At any rate my behaviour made von Uchri unsure of himself. It compelled him to say something about himself. He addressed the room, not me, with a voice that did not belong to him, almost choking.

"I am less than nothing. I want to repay everybody I like by pleasing them. Either out of vanity or need. But I have no attributes that are mine alone; only those belonging to others, that are mirrored in me. I am here simply as an unbidden guest."

I tried to stifle an inexplicable dread, got up, fetched two glasses from the sideboard along with the scarcely touched bottle of dark port.

"I like you," I said while pouring drinks for us both, "I feel that you are better suited to me than Manshard, who is leaving me — and Wagner, who I had chosen to be his successor a few hours ago."

I almost believe that my words gave him hope that he had not come in vain. I, for my part, was surprised by the resolution in what I said, but tried to convince myself I had not committed myself to anything. I sat down again in the assurance that this Ajax von Uchri would not leave immediately.

There was a lull in the conversation, which gave me time to muse on the newcomer's name: Ajax, son of Telamon, rescued Achilles from the Trojans; but when fork-tongued Odysseus wrested the victory from him during the argument over the dead man's weapons, Ajax succumbed to melancholy and killed himself.

During these thoughts, the living Ajax toyed with his full wine-glass, grasping the stem with the fingers of his one hand and slowly rotating it while his other hand remained motionless on the table like an animal waiting to pounce. This hand, this autonomous thing, was bony and quite large, well-groomed — yet covered in skin that was rough rather than smooth. I tried to compare it with hands that I knew. Suddenly it reminded me of that weather-beaten Lorraine peasant's hand belonging to Adam in the Church at Mont. I realised that this hand was likewise old, much older than the young man with his twenty-four years. It had cleared forests and diverted streams, carried stones and ploughed the land, whipped vassals and gutted deer, arduously plied a pen and battered wine goblets, fought, argued and delivered cowardly blows.

I hastily urged my guest to drink up. He raised his glass with his toying hand. The other remained motionless, as if it were not his, like a stone, no more precious nor less than a stone one picks up or leaves where it is.

And then the moment was over. I cleared my throat. We heard a loud spattering from the eaves.

"Herr Dumenehould died a man of honour. He had nothing to confess. I was with him in his final hour." Ajax von Uchri spoke the words all of a sudden, seemingly without forethought.

In retrospect I now feel he wished to dispel certain rumours and cast his own part in the man's fate in a better light. The shipping merchant had never made any bones about having an illegitimate son, he was after all unmarried. A couple of children whose father cannot be named, whom one might see playing on the street, resembled him; that was considered a fact. Down at the docks no one had forgotten the manly silhouette of a shipowner who boasted spawning nine and ninety bastards so as to breed good crews for his ships; apparently the old profligate had gathered them all around him shortly before he was carried to his red sandstone crypt.

"Did you see how he died? He must have been very wealthy, I presume?"

"A servant cannot estimate his master's riches," he swiftly replied, "he observes what kind of people frequent the house. He divines from the way the house is run, from the quality of the wines kept in the cellar, from the carpets and the paintings on the walls, from the size, the style and the number of the living-rooms, from the magnificence or selectness of the social occasions — from all this he divines the station of his employer."

"Fine," I said, "but you are still evading the question; I hope just for the moment. What I want you to do is to compare me with Herr Dumenehould. My house, my paintings, my park. Drink! Speak so that I may learn what expectations and experiences you have brought with you today. Tell me about the conditions of your employment there; the habits of masters and households differ, you know. After keeping silent for years on end, Manshard railed at me recently on account of my idiosyncrasies. I was quite defenceless; I realised I did not even know myself — as if I had no mirror image. So tell me!"

It seems that my clumsy words triggered something in Uchri's mind. He downed his glass. I filled it again. He took another drink. Then he was compliant and spoke.

"Apart from myself there were no menservants; a cook and a maid took care of day-to-day affairs. (I was their superior, but they detested me.) The house was cramped rather than roomy. A rather dingy hall and a large square room were kept for the occasional receptions. Hanging from the ceilings were prism chandeliers studded with candles. The floors were covered with several layers of carpets. Badly painted portraits and old seascapes decorated the walls which were papered with calico prints. Visitors had always to put up with the same ritual. Strong tea, buttered rolls and champagne were served. The number of chairs was never enough, so some of the guests would have to pass the hours either standing or seated on the floor. Apart from the frugal meal, music was also offered by the light of the flaming candles. Herr Dumenehould called the arrangements 'solemn' or even 'sublime'. The musicians were treated as equals among the guests. At a secret signal given by Herr Dumenehould, they stepped out from the crowd of those invited and magicked their instruments and sheet music from a corner. The piano virtuoso took his seat at the grand. Sometimes the music was just for violins and piano, but mostly there was a quartet or even a small orchestra."

He had risen from his chair so quietly that I did not notice at first. He stole as softly as a cat across the carpet, walking past my back so that the scent that enveloped him gently passed by me. A strange aroma of vanilla and tropical wood; perhaps simply a distillate of bergamot oil, not tangy, but not sickly. This and his behaviour excited me so that my perceptions were more hazy than focused. I readily forgot that we were strangers. In that moment I would have denied that a mire of unpredictability was perhaps about to open up before me. Our existence is as disparate as the crown of a tree whose leaves point at once towards the sun and the shade.

"Why are you wandering about the room?" I asked.

"It is a habit of mine," he replied, "it helps me remember more clearly. What people say is a mere excerpt. Everything is an excerpt; not only our knowledge and understanding — but also our memory, our chance actions. Each of us is just a drop in a blemished creation. I say something. I could say something different. So when I wander about a couple of images emerge from the shadows into the light. I study them. And I often don't like them."

"You were telling me about the conditions at the shipowner's house," I said, "and interrupted yourself."

Von Uchri returned to his chair, massaged the backrest for a few seconds with his hard fingers and sat down. As soon as I saw his hand back on the table, this old hand, this stone, I was overcome by a feeling of isolation, of vain endeavour, of separation. Each of us is a world or a void, cut off. Troubled, I waited for him to resume.

"In the latter years the guests were a mixed lot, more run–of–the–mill than select. A number of ageing gents gave the honour of their presence;

they were titled; but one could already make out their skulls, as if there were no flesh on them. I had to call them your grace, your excellence or Mr Senator. But they were clearly old dotards without any merit. Others were said to have written books, or to be gifted painters or sculptors, and formed a quarrelsome group; they shone by the loudness rather than the brilliance of their speech, drank deep of the champagne, and were not afraid to appear in red frock coats with golden braids or in morning suits, depending on whether they fancied themselves as snobs or as impoverished disciples of the arts. Herr Dumenehould de Rochemont singled them out from the other guests; the politeness he showed them had a heartfelt warmth. He never went so far as to buy a painting or a statue from one of these gentlemen, however much they pestered him and poured scorn on the 'junk', as they put it, hanging on his walls. He replied that his ancestors had managed to preserve their features even with the help of very mediocre painters, and that the ships done in their inks and oils had been depicted with such insight into their technical glory that the gentlemen artists could have no concept of their value. They were masterpieces, he said, and nor did they lack fantastical elements, in the form of ghosts, charmed from the sea floor by a spell. These generally noisy, boastful and dissatisfied guests were the faithful. They were rarely absent. I suspect that he gave them presents of money — or lent it to them, without it ever being repaid. It was his custom to remunerate his musicians by slipping them a sealed envelope just as they were on the point of leaving. He would also bestow similar gifts on his regulars, which they received like a tribute — not humbly but with their heads raised in pride. Obviously they would then shake his hand with a little more enthusiasm. There were also guests whom one saw but once and then never again, young men and women in the blossom of youth who were surrounded by the magic of anonymity — who everyone greeted with respect because no one knew who they were. Herr Dumenehould's brothers — he had two who both survived him — were never invited, or at least they never appeared; he probably had not even a scrap of fraternal respect for them. In their place came two fat ladies, the wives, one accompanied by a skinny son, the other led by a plump daughter. It is remarkable just how many fat or ugly women were to be seen at these functions. It seems that the receptions had no other purpose than to present a randomly selected group of people with the opportunity of listening together to the same works of music. The ship-owner met his business friends away from home at a restaurant. He explained to everyone who might be concerned and was willing to listen, that he had never had the good fortune to have a wife who would have made his house a cosy place to receive favoured guests; the sole attraction, he maintained, was a butler with an aristocratic title. An illegitimate son, who as the cook told me had been a frequent visitor to his father's house, and had died in their hands (as she put it) at the age of twenty. Although he had grown up in foreign parts, since time immemorial the son had kept his own room in the house, equipped with simple, childish treasures. It smelled of tarred ropes, and the cupboard drawers were full of curious objects. Minerals, desiccated animals, blocks of metal, cog-wheels that appeared to have been removed from some sort of machine or clock tower, cocoa beans, stamps, the skin flayed from a negro's back, boiled sweets and chocolate cakes. Attached to the walls were large tatters of bolted sail-cloth, pulleys, sealskins, ships' lamps, antlers cast by reindeer, model ships in liquor bottles, a turtle's shell. (He had hoped to become a ship operator like his father. Nobody could have known that he would have no future after his twentieth year.) Most of his stuff was still there when I commenced my employment. But his room had a smell like a section of a museum into which people rarely stray. He had been a first-rate swimmer and sailor, so it was said. One day between Christmas and New Year the ice on a pond broke beneath him. The result was a raging fever and pleurisy. He died in their hands. Herr Dumenehould engaged five doctors. When it was over and he was holding the body in his arms, all he said was: 'I was not meant to keep him.' The young man was interred in a walled crypt early in the morning, at 6 o'clock (it was still pitch black; some of the people carried torches so that they could see the way). Herr Dumenehould alone followed the coffin down the steep steps to the cellar. The pallbearers departed. The torches were planted in the ground. The shipowner remained for some time alone down there, until dawn broke and the workmen arrived to place a stone slab over the entrance."

Ajax von Uchri must have noticed as I wiped a couple of tears from my eye. He gave me a searching look.

"There is a similarity here. He also felt the pain that afflicted me," I said hesitantly.

Von Uchri noted my hint with detachment, as if it were of no consequence. And then he said something strange that appeared to have no purpose:

"The inner landscape does not differ much from person to person; the majority simply discipline nature by ploughing it up."

It was at that moment, at the latest, that I opened up to him. A resistance of I know not what kind towards this Ajax von Uchri suddenly dissolved. Everything that I have written until now is a summary I commenced after becoming aware of a melancholy attraction to him. It seems quite certain to me that he is neither upright nor honourable. But what kind of powers lend him his gentle deference, his feral naturalness, his grace and apparently motionless contemplation? A riven face with two fleshy landscapes. With its tired passion it seems almost beautiful.

"I am lonely," I tell him, "and probably a little mad. I can allow myself my little eccentric habits. I do not bother others with them; I live in seclusion. My life came to a stop in the past. I too had a son; admittedly he never grew to reach twenty. He died at the age of eight. He was my only child. My marriage only lasted two years. He was a pretty child. I loved him dearly. I still love him, as if he were alive: his image, his silenced voice. That is my madness, an inversion of my despair. In those days I always drove my car myself; it was a delight for me. One day a girl at play ran in front of the wheels. She died instantly. She lay there like a bundle. Her clothes were in disarray; but her head was uninjured. Her face was pale and frightened, but not distorted; framed by dark hair. One of her eyes was closed; the other continued to move, stared at me like a glass eye that does not see, staring. Then it closed. I picked her up, carried her to my car. Later I discovered a small pool of blood on the cushions. No, the accident was not my fault; no one could accuse me, not even I myself. A few weeks later my boy was mangled underneath an automobile that was driven by a drunk. He was struck while walking along the pavement, knocked over. His head was smashed, but there was not a scratch on his pretty body…"

"There is no connection," said Ajax von Uchri, "morality is an accessory. Thousands are killed every day, on the streets, in the mines, in the factories, or as wretches who die of hunger or corruption; hundreds of thousands die because their time is up. All attempts to explain this tragedy arrive at false conclusions. The course of events is bound to an inexorable law, not to morals. Religions and nations, which foster millions of murders, collapse after a few centuries, but not because revenge is taken on them for their crimes. Their avengers are other people who for their part are also to be numbered among the murderers. Man has only an imaginary soul; instead of true existence he has a mind that allows itself to be led astray — that seems to exist solely to be led astray, rather than to correct creation by its compassion."

"But I was dealt an unexpected blow," I replied, "my love for the small pretty body, which was the form of forms for me, can never be expunged. I have pictures, a bronze cast, and a head full of memories. I can no longer drive the car since he, Olav, was cut off so young. It was not the death of the girl that caused this paralysis in me. Fate's pronouncements are a closed book to me, the mythology of chance fills me with fruitless horror."

"Human life is an artistic construction, not a steaming mass. Animals do not know death, at most dying. We alone are cursed with knowledge of it. There are untold millions of pretty eight-year-old boys; but your mind suppresses that. You do not wish to recognise life in its massive extension."

As he spoke I saw that his features communicated something other than what he was saying. He turned as pale as ash, then immobile, so impassive that the last creases in his forehead disappeared. His eyelids closed; evidently visions were forming behind them that had no place in my room.

"I cannot drive a car," he said, unexpectedly, "I shall have to learn."

"Did you shave Herr Dumenehould every day?" I asked.

"Never; but I expect that I will not prove unskilled in the matter."

"You scarcely have any of the accomplishments that are required here."

"I have others. From time to time I can get to grips with harsh realities, with the severity of creation, because I do not believe in a life that offers the possibility of a certain duration. I take up an unremitting struggle in order still to be here the next day; but I assume that every day is my last. Which is why I am dependable, capable of anything and completely amenable."

I was taken aback. Simultaneously I felt pity for him, for myself, for humanity, an indistinct feeling. Being capable of everything, is that not the ultimate accomplishment, the final assurance that more malleable stuff is present inside us? Is not anarchy the last bastion before the absolute sovereignty of the bureaucracies — in which there is no compassion, no turning back, no justice, only judges, a progressive stripping of the senses and death to the spirit; where production takes the place of creation, mass experience that of happiness?

"The great herd of soldiers must stake their lives, and yet there is scarcely a hero among them. Workers in the mines and at rapacious machines are exposed to danger. Discipline was invented by rulers. Not much has changed in creation since the beginning. Wolves and gods still wander the earth, hungry and in search of prey. Sacrifices are made to them; but the bowels of the earth continue to devour. We cannot appease or propitiate the unknown powers. Nor should we believe that justice or fairness exist. And neither should we attempt to learn the truth. All that we search for is hidden in another reality, not here."

I interrupted him, and once again unfolded the letter bearing the ship-owner's praises.

"When did Herr Dumenehould de Rochemont write this little reference for you?"

"On the day of his death."

"Did he die suddenly?"

"He was a marked man. He was already past his time. He managed to defy fate for a brief moment — so — so as to die in his own way."

"How am I to understand that? We have already discussed a number of things, Herr von Uchri; I am not unwilling to trust you; but your otherness, your youth, if you like, dismays me. You have convinced me with your openness, but I fear you might begin to lie without reason, or seek some advantage by lying."

He laughed.

"Yes, lying is often our safest refuge. We have to accept all of our lot as experience. We must accept our waxing and waning, and the dread disappointment that we cease to be anything when we come to be marked by our predispositions, by an accident or age. And who of us is free of predispositions that displease others? I think there are adverse circumstances in which our only consolation is a lie. We are cosseted and comforted in the real, deep and all-embracing lie. There no one can find us, not even we ourselves. It is an exodus to another star. In the final count these walkers of the galaxies are not up to much either. If it is necessary to lie, I lie. If I wish to commend myself, I must be open, for otherwise I am cheating. After all, one takes rotten eggs back to the tradesman."

"Fine, von Uchri. I asked you to tell me about Herr Dumenehould's death."

"He suffered from angina pectoris, spasms of the heart. It is an unabating, futile battle with extinction. The fear in one's breast tries to outdo the pain, and pain the fear. The machine fails, which the mind registers with brutal clarity. In vain the hand presses itself to the spot where the pain is rooted. Incidentally, it begins, curiously enough, in the left shoulder. From there it reaches right into the heart, right into the soul. There is no deliverance from it, just a postponement of the final judgement. The pain can be allayed just so many times, and the fear with it, by means of one of those mysterious capsules. After every crisis, except the last, there is relief. But the patient is aware that once his veins have grown brittle with age, he has nothing to hope for any more. At any rate Herr Dumenehould knew from a certain moment just where he stood. He calculated on the basis of his experience that he would die in a fit of mortal terror of merciless dimensions, quite independent of his readiness to die. He wanted to elude this terrible, this natural death. He did not reach his decision hastily. An old man loves every single day of his life. We talked about it. After a serious attack it was time to take action. He needed my help. He wanted to hold one last pleasant picture before his mind's eye. He put some of his papers in order. But I know very little about that. One evening he dressed as if for a large festive reception and lay down on the bed in the tall room with the white ceiling and the walls covered in grey floral silk. 'I am ready,' he said to me. I went to the bathroom next door, so as to transform what is visibly me for the solemn occasion. Divested of all my clothing, but rubbed down all over with English red and like a devil or an angel in appearance, unrecognisable but for the mould of my own form, I re-entered the bedroom. 'I like you like that,' Herr Dumenehould said, 'but don't say a word. Do not reveal who you are. I do not want to know you. The syringe is on the bedside cabinet. I have counted out a hundred pounds for you. Stay with me until my eyes close. There is nothing more to say.' He pushed up the sleeve of his coat himself, so that I could insert the needle under the skin of his arm. The shock set in, heavy, stertorous breathing. For a while he looked at me in astonishment, his face flushed. And then his eyes actually closed. I crept back to the bathroom and spent an hour soaping myself, bathing and showering so as to remove the powder from my hair and skin. After I had dressed and returned to the bedroom, Herr Dumenehould was no longer breathing. I took his hand. He had taken off a ring and buried it in his fist, a ring with a heavy, green shimmering diamond. That must have been his last deed. He knew that I would steal the ring. He owed me the opportunity. I took it. I went downstairs to the shipowner's office. I picked up the telephone and told one of Herr Dumenehould's brothers that my master was dead."

I allowed Ajax to tell his story without interrupting him even once. It struck me as unreal — as if one were looking with wakeful eye upon the face of a water sprite at the bottom of a pond. Other lives, other pasts which we can only picture to ourselves in words, not in their own time — which we would have dealt with differently, or in which we did not even exist — such lives have something abstract, something monstrous about them, that cannot fully be grasped. But I did not doubt the truth of his words. My hands began to shake, I said: "You were paid for your services, I suppose? The shipowner gave you one hundred English pounds? Did he not have any heirs? Was he never married? Had he a brother, or several of them? Did he die a rich man?"

"Although there was no reliable evidence I nevertheless assumed that he was rich." Ajax von Uchri spoke with uncertainty.

I said: "He was rich, he was exceptionally rich. A hundred pounds was a measly payment."

"It was an appropriate sum," von Uchri said, "we negotiated it between ourselves. The work took me only two hours of my time."

"But he was rich," I said, "his death was to be sweetened. Perhaps he even managed to remember his son with complete clarity. He did not have any heirs. Or are you hiding the fact that he remembered you in his will?"

"I did not mean anything to him after his death. Once he had expired he wanted the conventions he had disregarded during his lifetime to come into their own. His family, which he had despised, his brothers, were to take care of his body. He left nothing to me; apart from a recommendation. No one can jump over their own shadow. He had loved the ships and the painted figures of his ancestors on the walls. A rich man will never hit on the idea of placing his servant on the same footing, not even after his own metamorphosis. He had long since weighed him up, he knew the value of his inferiors. Their value lies in their usefulness. There is a difference between a lackey and an illegitimate son. The natural son can have the look of one of those painted forbears. Any number of princes have extolled their bastards, but only a few have placed their servants above their hounds. He knew that I would steal his diamond ring. He had already removed it from his finger months before and carried it in his waistcoat pocket — so that no one who met him would notice the gem and later remember that it had still been in his possession shortly before his death. Not until his dying day did he place the ring back on his hand — and then slipped it off before he hastened to his death."

"If he knew that you would steal the diamond," I asked excitedly, "and this theft had his consent, why didn't he make you a present of the stone?"

"He realised that no one would believe I was the lawful owner. Knowing I was in my right, I might have been careless enough to wear the ring in public, and no sooner had I done so than the police would be called in. A poor person is always under suspicion. That is the way the rich have arranged things."

"But he had written a will, he could have included the bequest." (I wanted to clear up this theft. I don't know why exactly. Sometimes I am a little bit pedantic.)

"A will extends beyond death; it is something solemn, something historical. Can't you understand? People are reluctant to refer back in it to their life, which, however it may have been, is over — or assumed to be finished. On paper the stone would have turned into money. In life it was an adornment, a jewel that granted its owner prestige. The prestige of a negro chief or the wearer of a medal."

"And yet I still do not understand why he wanted to make a thief of you," I said, "why he didn't find a way round it."

"He simply didn't want to. He wanted yet one more experience after death. A contact. I was to prize open his cooling hand. He cherished feelings of friendship or admiration for a thief. Similar to the horror and delight of licentious love. Did it not occur to him in the last seconds of his life that I might cut off his fingers?"

I have described our conversation with as much veracity as I can summon, albeit probably slightly abridged because the time needed to write is longer than that needed to speak. Ajax von Uchri's character revealed itself as increasingly intricate with every sentence; this twenty-four-year-old became uncanny and simple, criminal and good in equal measure. I do not know why he was so talkative; he could have remained silent about a lot of things, without any risk of being caught out; there were, after all, no witnesses to speak against him.

It took an absurd audacity to entrust me with all this, but evidently I am a suitable person for such dangerous confidences. I no longer sense the power of my nature — I do not have a clear-cut character, in the way we say that people have. I savoured the natural in him, the dubious, his inevitability, like an incomprehensible miracle. Even now I cannot free myself of a solemn feeling of apprehension.

He is not much of a thief, he is simply capable of everything. Even if I do not yet know him at all. He is a different person from the one he professed to be today. In fact I have already forgotten the exact expression on his face when he related how he had been painted red to become the angel of death. Paint ousts the flesh. The mask has more permanence than our shifting reality. A mummy is more persistent than life.

My heart beats fitfully; I recognise my gaucheness, my inability to come to a decision — my anxiety about entrusting myself to life, which is to say to people and indeed to a single person. I am afraid that one day this Ajax will bring home a pretty eight-year-old boy, of which there are millions, as he says — in order to render ineffective the brazen mummy, that cheap copy of a dead person. And I will be quite defenceless.

I must write him or Wagner a letter retracting my offer.

Regrettably my nerves baulk at the prospect. My brain is occupied with all manner of nonsense; nor is it made to record my every feeling correctly; it constantly changes things, and now I too have undergone a change. I have shown him, this Ajax von Uchri, the images and the bronze body lying there; I removed the black velvet canopy. He saw this, all that remains of Olav.

"It is beautiful," he said, "but completely hard."

I replaced the black cover and replied, saying that I would like him to be my servant.

He looked at me, furtively, to see whether I had really meant it; or if I was dependable enough that he and I could find a common purpose.

He decided quickly. He reached into his trouser pocket and pulled out the ring he had talked about. A simple white band with an unusually large sparkling stone instilled with the green swell of a chill evening sky. I took a step back.

"I am surprised that the diamond is so large," I stuttered.

"It is worth twenty thousand krones or more — under the counter," von Uchri replied, "but it is hard to sell. I do not have a certificate of provenance. I have made enquiries. It has a pedigree. It is what is known as a solitaire, a fantasy stone."

The ring slipped back into Ajax von Uchri's pocket.

"So you agree to take me?" he asked.

I had a presentiment that my voice would sound ill-natured when I spoke. Self-consciousness and naked astonishment had instantly lodged in my larynx, which was bound to engender misunderstandings. I cleared my throat.

"You are not exactly being polite," he said bitterly after a while, "and I was foolish enough to demonstrate the truth about my past."

I gave in at once. I did not wish to seem mean. I tried to give him some notion of the vagaries of my larynx.

"I ask you to give me a month's wages right now in advance, to show that you are in earnest."

I gave him the money. That action decided to whom I will address the letter of retraction.

The Night of Lead

"I'm leaving you now. You must continue on your own. You must explore this town which you do not know." Matthieu, who had kept his head bowed, looked up. He recognised that it was night — a black sky with no stars; that there were houses, cobbled streets; that he was standing on a corner, where the paving stones met under his feet from two directions; that a harsh yellow light, emanating from the lamps suspended high above, illuminated the scene, this new scene, this street corner and a wide boulevard which he could look down in both directions. Shiny tramlines, embedded in the cobble-stones, appeared from far away, vanished far away, straight as a die, it seemed to him, in the incessant yellow glare that shone from the innumerable lights suspended above.

While his mind prepared itself to be astonished, he sensed that he wore no clothes and was thus an unseemly blot on the street. Yet he felt this nakedness only for a few seconds. He moved his arms, expanded his chest. He leaned back against the air that surrounded him, and felt that it supported him. He recognised the tone of the voice, the body that had yet to bid him farewell. He felt the kindly warmth from that other person, touched with his skin the form that was clinging to him, comprehended — with overpowering clarity — that this being, masculine, was holding him with its whole frame.

Then it was gone — brushed away like the voice. Matthieu reeled. He looked back. He was abandoned. He stood there in his clothes, ordinary, an indecisive person.

"I have the choice of either left or right. So which way shall I go, because I am a stranger here without a home, and know no one who could advise me?"

He took a few steps forward so as to better estimate the length of the boulevard, perhaps discover an end or a curve. But there were no bounds to the glistening rails that he could see, nor an end to the number of lamps. It was like the space between two gigantic mirrors facing one another — an infinity which one may calculate but not believe. And he saw no people, try as he could to find his like. The façades were lit up, and appeared a uniform colour in the light, some being simply coated in shadows or muddied with dirt. Up above, the buildings disappeared in the black of the boundless sky. And every door and window was black, as if they were holes in front of the void.

Matthieu discovered a single illuminated window in the distance. This decided him to take that direction. He did not expect anything from the window; but gradually his steps grew resolute, as if they had a goal.

As he walked he was more and more astonished not to meet anyone, not a living soul, not a fellow being. There was also no sound, no noise. The buildings were hushed and the air motionless.

"What time must it be for such a large town to be asleep, as if it were not a town but a field somewhere in the dark? And why are the street lights illuminated when there is no traffic?"

He answered himself, by reflecting that he knew nothing of the customs of the inhabitants. And since he was not tired, he was unconcerned that he had no home. Nevertheless he made for the window with more haste — as if it had some meaning for him.

Then he stood before the building which had drawn him. The glimmering window was on the second floor. He looked up. The light, diffusing through the curtains, suggested a snug room — domestic seclusion — warmth; yet simultaneously abandonment, the loneliness of a solitary life.

"There is only one person behind the window. There is a similarity with myself. I do not know him. He does not know me. I could go up to him…"

Matthieu, his head cast back, stared at the comforting rectangle in the otherwise blank, expressionless face of the building. A longing awoke in him, a desire for fellowship, impatience, audacity — the audacity to penetrate this building, to accost someone from this town, the first person of whom he had found any trace, to make his acquaintance.

Every memory he had brought from other towns seemed to have deserted him. All he knew now was himself, the sensations of these moments. Animate life was all that he felt, by no means clearly, beneath his clothes: a slight warmth, some abstruse sort of behaviour. Nothing seemed to resemble the mirror image that he created of himself obeying a confused urge.

He spoke out loud: "The inner experiences of all the inhabitants of this town are quite unlike mine." And after a while: "We walk the streets until our love turns bad."

With that he took a step towards the front door, determined to clasp the door handle and gain entry, if need be by force or skill.

In that very moment the window went dark, became as black as the others in this façade and the thousands of others dotting this long-extending avenue. And with the window, the street lights extinguished too; or rather they now merely glowed without producing any appreciable light. It was as if a pall of black smoke had descended.

Matthieu immediately dismissed the idea of entering the building. In fact for a moment he saw nothing.

"It was the last lit window in this town tonight. Now there is no more need of illuminated streets. The town squandered the light because one last person indicated that they were not asleep. Everyone, even if they remain awake from now on, is in the dark or behind black bulkheads or in windowless cellars."

Strangely he soon felt certain that not all of the inhabitants had succumbed to sleep — as little as had he — and that these sleepless people hidden wherever they were would resemble him — that he was one of them. The window whose light had drawn him became unimportant. On looking up again, he could no longer tell which of the dead black eyes had still been alive a moment ago.

He noted with satisfaction that the outlines of the buildings, pavement and road were once again recognisable now that he had grown accustomed to the lack of light. He carried on, in the opposite direction to the one in which he had come. His thoughts were neither sharp nor intrusive. He might have described himself as drowsy, but not tired, simply inattentive, quite indifferent to his condition and the sombre town — everything was blurred. "We walk the streets until our love turns bad," he thought once more.

The sentence meant nothing more to him than the unnecessary realisation that he was a grown-up person and capable of grown-up feelings.

After some time he regretted not having forced his way into the house. "The person would not yet have been asleep," he observed. "I could have sat on the edge of the bed, we could have talked or questioned each other."

This imaginary encounter did not assume any firm contours. He pictured neither a man nor a woman, and children did not even occur to him. He merely regretted his lack of determination. He resolved not to waste the next opportunity. Admittedly the thought crossed his mind once again that the people he might encounter now must be like him: restless, sleepless, unlike the long-established residents who were all asleep — and who therefore must differ from those who were awake.

Matthieu tried to find a way to express this difference in his mind. But regardless of what image he conjured up, it became blurred. Those who were asleep merged with those awake, acquired a single identity with his own self, an unseemly one, as if the whole world were Matthieu, this grown-up person with grown-up person feelings, twenty-three years old, who had not yet needed to think about his death, who had a past of twenty-three years, an insubstantial past. A small desire for love had grown in him; but the favour had yet to be bestowed upon him. He walked on down the streets because these twenty-three years had been so ordinary, not happy. Some went with women, others with youths. That much was known. The rest was business, boredom, art, St. Peter's Cathedral, pyramids, Bach, Ockeghem or Stravinsky, kitsch or Shakespeare, God or cosmos. Glossy magazines replaced minds. Gaga. They were buried or cremated. Without exception.

Annoyed, he said: "I have let an opportunity slip away to get to know the real inhabitants. It is too difficult for me to imagine the sleep of all these strangers. All I know is that they are lying there; but for me they have no face. Do they know the poet Pythagoras or the medusa Tukki? Have they put their heads between their thighs and raised their hats to their backsides? I should at least have studied a face, for you can't imagine a cat's head when you've never seen a cat; at best one would end up with a toad or a pancake. And I have never seen them..."

He stumbled. The sound of stone and shoe-sole rang out like the crack of a whip. The sound was echoed by the building on the other side of the street.

"Now they know I am here," he said, "now I have been heard."

He carried on, filled with a kind of confidence. At least the silence had been rent.

But nothing happened. Not a window opened, no one stepped outside, there were no shouts.

"Everyone is sound asleep," he said, and he carried on hastily, as if he had to reach a destination as soon as possible.

Then a man stopped him. He had stepped from a doorway and blocked the way.

Matthieu could not identify at first who was obstructing him. He merely started, spoke an ill-considered word. The man's contour indicated a large, broad figure, corpulence and power. Matthieu also thought he could make out a uniform of sorts; at any rate the stranger's clothing had shiny buttons. But until he spoke it was merely an assumption that this was a man. The figure switched on a torch, handed Matthieu a card and illuminated it so that he could read what was printed on it. After some hesitation Matthieu resolved to decipher the text. He read:

Elvira will receive you in charming salons. Sandwiches. Wines. Lovely breasts. Unique transformations. Single donation of 50 francs. No one will regret having helped Elvira.

The torch was switched off; Matthieu kept the card in his hand. (Later it got lost; he probably threw it away.)

"Are you the doorman here?" he asked.

"I am whatever you care to call me, sir," replied the figure in a deep voice.

"Who is Elvira?" Matthieu asked.

"A surprise," said the porter.

"That is vague," said Matthieu.

"You cannot know anything before you have had the experience," said the porter.

"Such talk is of no interest to me," said Matthieu, "I wish to continue on my way."

"You are mistaken, sir, you do not wish to continue on your way. You have come to this town and cannot pass by here. You know as much yourself. You have an obligation. You have already missed out on a lot. You missed out on the lit window."

The figure forced Matthieu, who still resisted, sideways. It did not touch him; but the shadow of its outline acted on him like a force.

Matthieu spoke again: "I know nothing about you; but you know something about me. It is true that I did not avail myself of the lit window. Afterwards I resolved not to miss another opportunity. But I have the impression that I am simply being detained here, that my goal is elsewhere."

"As you wish, sir," came the deep voice, "there is no compulsion. You may pass over as many opportunities to experience something as you wish. But at some point the town comes to an end. Please remember that, sir! Suddenly you will find yourself in a deserted field — with the town behind you. You will be unable to turn back. All that will remain is your regret at not having learnt anything about the inhabitants. There is no turning back here — always just one direction. I shall lock the door in a few minutes. Then it will be too late for anyone who wishes to enter. There will be no more admission."

He started to return to the doorway.

"Please, stay a moment with me," said Matthieu, "I am a stranger here and realise of course that I am doing some things wrong; but if you were to explain these customs which are new to me in more depth, I would become less gauche."

"You may accompany me. I am not permitted to stand on the street too long. You must accept that without explanation. It is a rule. It is quite irrelevant whether it is linked to some reasonable purpose or is an old regulation whose meaning has been forgotten. One doesn't question such matters."

Matthieu wanted to raise an objection; but he quickly decided not to be so stubborn. He took a couple of steps towards the porter.

"It's easy to come this way," the latter said by way of encouragement.

"You must lead me," said Matthieu, for he felt as though he was slowly going blind.

The porter took him by the arm. At first Matthieu was tugged gently. But as the darkness beyond the doorway became impenetrable — the door had swung open with a gentle wafting motion and fallen to with a grating sound — the two shuffled along side by side like friends. Matthieu trusted that his companion would draw his attention to a step, say, or an unevenness in the ground. And if he tripped, the man's strong arm, which was clasped gently round his shoulder, would prevent him from falling. The porter also seemed to find his way in the darkness, much to Matthieu's surprise, for he sensed only blackness with no direction. There was doubtless a rule that the torch should not be switched on — and a reason for this which was not directly accessible. Matthieu tried to trace a thought, to shape a memory. He did not succeed. He was not afraid; nor did he have any expectations. He forgot how he had come to be in this darkness.

The porter told him to stand still and removed the protection of his arm. Matthieu heard him take a few more steps, followed by the sound of a key being turned. A door was unlocked. And light issued through the opening door.

An unspeakable feeling of happiness flooded through Matthieu. The light was not harsh and dazzling, but a dull warm glow. It did not make Matthieu squint. He walked to the door. He saw the doorman standing there, magnificent, gold-braided like an admiral, drawn up to his full height, his hand raised to his hat...

"Here we part ways," said the man, "I shall remain here. You must go up the stairs."

Matthieu remained a moment, undecided, wondered whether he owed his companion a tip, reached into his pocket, realised that he had no money on him, blushed.

"You must go up the stairs," the doorman repeated.

Still confused, Matthieu took a few hesitant steps, came to a spacious hallway. He wanted to ask the portly man another question, excuse himself; but the door slammed shut.

"In that other house I would have had to climb the stairs without any instruction," he thought fleetingly, now that he was left on his own.

Then he concentrated on what he could see.

At first he studied the lamp. It was fashioned with three arms, a candelabrum bearing three candles with lively red flames; the bronze stand was decorated with cut-glass figures and prisms, smoke-coloured lead crystal which sparkled and now and then turned the light into a rainbow of colours.

The hallway was an elongated octagon. The staircase to the upper floor was half spiraliform, with the bottom steps set at the back. There was also a descending staircase, with ornate carved wooden banisters similar to those leading upwards, which awakened the impression of not being at ground level... The walls were covered with pastel-coloured stucco decorations, as if a master builder from the Baroque era had constructed the house. Matthieu felt a warmth in his heart. Apart from the entrance, he was unable to detect any openings in the walls. He considered testing whether the door behind him had been locked; he decided not to do so.

As he languidly mounted the ascending staircase, he no longer had any reservations — regardless of what he might encounter. He was merely surprised that his heart did not beat faster with excitement, as if nothing was awaiting him. A hide of dead leather would have been no less indifferent than his living body.

The upper hallway resembled the one below in every detail. Here, too, there was a door — and the staircase repeated itself, so that Matthieu doubted whether he had even moved. In order to make certain, he opened the door through which, had he been but only in a dream, he must have come.

Instead of blackness washing towards him there came perfume, warmth, and a golden light, sparkling with colour. He saw a sumptuous, lavishly appointed room; but more important, a handsome young person, a groom in a grey uniform.

The groom bowed, took Matthieu's hat, gestured to show him the right way, and said, with a high, clear voice, as if he were not even fifteen years old:

"Welcome, sir!"

Matthieu was not surprised; he simply looked at the graceful figure with delight.

"What's your name?" he asked.

"Franz, sir — or Donkey; I'm called that too because I am dressed in grey."

"I am a stranger here... Donkey, that's a good name," said Matthieu. He stopped talking; he felt awkward and in need of help. He repeated, almost in a whisper: "I am a stranger here."

"I know, sir. Trust me. I shall be at your side, so that you won't make a wrong move. Apart from that, there are no rules in this house. Everyone behaves as they wish. You may greet me by shaking my hand or by giving me a kiss or unbuttoning my litevka, according to your inclinations or promptings. No one will be offended."

Matthieu did not reply. He studied the young man. "He really does have a pretty mouth," the older man observed. Yet he found the prettiest thing about him was his lush yellow-blond hair, on which the grey woollen cap sat at such an angle that it remained a mystery why it did not fall off — and there was no strap to secure it. Matthieu touched the hair with sudden tenderness.

"You have already started to learn, sir," said the groom. "You are acting according to your promptings. But you should have stroked me firmly, as if I were a real donkey."

Matthieu considered whether he should answer. He had seen the youth's pale eyes light up with joy, like fanned coals — and straight after extinguish, become as grey as ashes.

"What a pity — this grace fades so quickly," he said, very softly.

"It has already faded, sir, for yesterday I was more graceful, and the day before even more graceful, and the day before that yet more graceful still — and so on, back to the beginning, many months ago…"

"No," said Matthieu briefly, "you are still handsome." He took off his overcoat.

"You will learn, sir," said the groom as he took the garment and carried it to an adjoining room.

For a while Matthieu was alone. He stood on the bare parquet floor. He turned round in a circle, slowly, to gain a clearer idea of his surroundings. At first he had only had the diffuse impression of gold and colour; the groom's sweet appearance had immediately captivated his senses, so his picture of the room had remained incomplete; now he saw that large paintings were hanging on the chintz-lined walls, reaching almost from the floor to the ceiling. They depicted landscapes in shades of green, brown and blue, and were mounted in magnificent gold frames. Standing on ornately turned golden legs in front of them were several short, upholstered benches covered in blue silk. A crystal chandelier, larger and more splendid than those on the landings, illuminated the room.

Matthieu was just about to sit on one of the benches when Donkey, the groom, returned. Matthieu now discovered a light blond down on the youth's opulent, almost swollen-looking red lips, the seductive discord between lugubrious development and final perfection — and smiled.

"I would like to see your hands," he said abruptly, "now that I know your face."

The youth went to him and presented his hands; first the palms, then the backs. Matthieu studied them carefully, grasped the hands, held them, turned them to the left and right.

"You are an able person," he said, "you have good hands. They are clear, simple, pleasing, nicely shaped — neither too long nor too coarse."

"Yesterday they were more pleasing, sir, the day before even more pleasing, the day before that yet more pleasing — and so on, back to the beginning many months ago..."

"You are a foolish Donkey," said Matthieu, letting the hands slip from his own.

"You will learn, sir," said the groom, "but I do not begrudge your thinking well of me. Because both what is permitted and what is evil issues from the same substance, from the flesh. Deadening self-denial begins first in unreality. Everything which is real is true. The visible only deceives on the surface. The invisible cannot be examined. It is elusive. The elusive is the cause of our fears."

"Are those your words?" Matthieu asked, alarmed.

The youth smiled, pouting his full lips even more than when he spoke.

"All words are old. Who do they actually belong to? They have a meaning which conveys very little. All that ever belongs to us is this life. Activity is our renunciation. Didn't you know that?"

Matthieu felt as though he was being touched by icy hands. He tried to shake off what he was encountering, but the strange dimension in which he had landed clung to him; suddenly a frosty presence.

"Why am I here in fact?" he asked, distracted.

"You have been talking with me, sir," the groom returned. "Half an hour ago you didn't know me, were unaware of my existence. You could not have suspected that I have this form and this constitution. But you still know little about me, for you have not kissed me, have not unbuttoned my litevka. Perhaps my lips are frozen quicksilver and my chest…"

"One shouldn't play with words in such a revolting manner," Matthieu interjected. "Red lips are warm; we know that from experience. I know that red lips… that a person's chest… it's the most certain…"

"Please, sir, forget our conversation! Forgive my impropriety! I have ventured too far. I have been talking nonsense. I shall now announce you to the lady of the house."

"Yes," said Matthieu, and he felt the faint iciness depart, "that's why I came. I had forgotten."

The groom opened one of the broad double doors set in the wall between two paintings of sweeping trees, dogs and archaic ruins. He announced to the neighbouring room: "Mr Matthieu has arrived."

Matthieu did not recall mentioning his name, but he was happy that he had lost some of his anonymity without any effort on his part. He heard a woman's voice answer the groom: "Please show him in."

He stepped through the door which Donkey opened extra wide and then closed behind him.

He felt at once that he had gone the wrong way, or was only in an antechamber. He had heard the voice, but could see no one, although the room was easy to take in: rectangular, with only a few pieces of furniture. There were a couple of chairs, a divan, a standard lamp, a large carpet — but neither a table nor a cupboard. Apart from the door through which he had entered, there did not seem to be another.

He cleared his throat, but this prompted no response. Matthieu now walked across the carpet to the centre of the room. He noticed clearly that it had no window, and recalled that the stairwell and the room in which he had talked with the groom had exhibited a similarly curious hermeticism from the outside world. He sought an explanation for this singular fact, but his reflections bore no fruit.

Suddenly the wall opened, or rather, a concealed door opened just at the place at which Matthieu was staring. He took a step back, less alarmed than surprised. A woman, young, dressed in a long green silk gown, was smiling at him. She remained in the doorway for a moment, as if waiting for Matthieu's astonishment to dissipate. Even after she had taken the first steps towards him, and the hidden door had closed behind her as if by a breeze, her smile, which lacked any intrinsic expression, remained on her lips; and she did not speak a word.

Matthieu bowed; but this gesture was neither noticed nor acknowledged, and was not returned in any way. He then tried to justify his presence with another bow, and by referring to the fleeting invitation on the street and all the other coincidences that seemed worthy of mention. He felt though that his account amounted to little, particularly because he did not mention the card which the doorman had given him, for he was embarrassed that he no longer had it.

"Please don't mention such trifles, Matthieu," the woman interrupted. "I am Elvira; that is the explanation for everything. Since I never go to anybody, they must come to me. Forget for the present your journey, and where you have come from. Your memories are anyway false. You wish to give purpose to your plan and to arrange your past so that it becomes meaningful. That's a pretty game — nothing more. You have lived fleetingly; which is to say: you have made yourself at home in your body. I doubt though whether you have developed much taste in the process. At any rate, looking at you one immediately gets the impression that you do not know where is the bed within you."

Matthieu attempted a laugh, without success.

"I experience myself as if in a mist, unclear, expressionless — as if I had swallowed a narcotising poison. My past is already so fragmentary that I would shudder were I fully in command of my senses..." He thought it, he did not speak it.

"You are gauche," said Elvira, "I would like to remind you that you received my card and read it. So... why are you here?"

"To see you, Elvira," he said briefly.

"That is the first sensible sentence you have spoken, Matthieu. For 50 francs one gets to see a person, regardless of what the town is called and where it is located; whether it is day or night."

She clapped her hands. Donkey, the groom, appeared at once at the door. "Are you ready?" he asked.

"Please serve," said Elvira, with another clap.

Donkey entered, took two chairs from against the wall and placed them on the carpet in the middle of the room.

He also placed the standard lamp beside them. Then he scurried out of the room only to return a second later pushing a table on castors, set with plates and cutlery, glasses and sandwiches.

"I assume you drink champagne," said Elvira.

She did not await Matthieu's confirmation, but ordered the groom to fetch a bottle at once.

After the wine had also been brought in, Donkey retired and Elvira and Matthieu sat at the table opposite each other, lit by the standard lamp.

Only now did Matthieu study the woman more closely; she also looked at him, but unobtrusively. He, however, could not conceal his challenging inquisitiveness.

Elvira seemed to become more youthful by the minute. When she appeared in the hidden doorway he had guessed she was thirty. Now he subtracted several years. After staring at her face for a while — with unseemly persistence — these years became a decade. This face, in that first moment he would have called it gracious, now appeared to be exceptionally beautiful. He felt sure that Elvira was the groom's sister, but she was much lovelier than the pretty youth. Matthieu became infatuated by her mouth which, slightly open, was turned directly towards him, denuded, as it were, but without offering itself. At first they did not look each other in the eyes. Now their gazes met. Matthieu bent forward and studied Elvira's hands. "Those are Donkey's hands. She is his sister." His confusion grew. He struggled in the grip of passion, but his thoughts were poor guardians against the reckless and overwhelming desire that filled his being.

Elvira helped him pacify the tumult once more. She asked him, rather casually:

"Tell me, Matthieu, do you think my make-up is too heavy?"

He raised his head, perplexed. And saw that her face was covered with a layer of matter, the suggestion of a form that was not her skin. He had not noticed until then. It sobered him, but for no substantial duration. He did not reply. She placed a few titbits before him. This prompted him to fill the glasses.

"I do not feel any hunger," he said.

"Anyone who does not like food and drink is in danger, whether they know it or not," she said.

He fell silent. They toasted one another. Matthieu noted that his sense of taste was absent; at least, he did not feel the tingle of the wine. Confused, he placed a morsel in his mouth and sensed no more than his own saliva — or the slightly salty addition of blood. He felt as though his stomach did not exist. He ate nothing more.

"Don't you like it?" asked Elvira.

At first he lied, saying that he found the wine and food excellent; then he admitted that they tasted insipid.

"It tastes like soda water to me, like soda water," he said to his own amazement.

"I'm sorry about that," she replied calmly, "I conclude from this that the danger you are in is great, that it threatens your life. The food is as excellent as it looks. And the champagne is better than iced water."

"This slight disability of my palate is quite unimportant..." He tried to calm himself and dispel the discomfort his hostess must be feeling. Both seemed to succeed; at any rate she no longer urged him to eat and drink. As for himself, he soon forgot the disappointment of his tongue. Even her words about danger withered into something to be cast aside.

He studied Elvira's dress, the olive-green silk and its cut. He could not see the train, because they were seated at the table. The sleek, tight-fitting top revealed a well-proportioned figure, a perfection for which he knew no comparison. Her neck, white, covered by soft shadows, was enclosed by a tall collar which opened stiffly at the front and led to an unobtrusive slit which disappeared between her breasts. It was no more than a hint of a slit, lined with material. But Matthieu's imagination had been stirred, and he found the arrangement of the material congruent with his wishes. The cut promised something, fired his slightly timid passion and made bold his speech.

"May I sit beside you, Elvira?" he asked, blushing.

"It is natural that you should ask as much, now that you have stopped eating and drinking," she said.

With these words she turned down the collar of her dress; the slit opened as naturally as if a loose veil had simply been whisked aside. The beautiful symmetry of Elvira's breasts was revealed. A benign creation seemed to have formed them with indescribable care — watching over their gradual development, overlooking none of the mysteries of their preordained perfection nor over-hastily forgetting their outward grace or delicacy.

The Night of Lead

Matthieu leapt up, wounded by a sort of delirium, sharp as a dagger. It was a stab to the centre of his flesh, he felt the wound gape open, the spurt of blood.

"Elvira!" he shouted, enraptured, half fainting, "— Elvira. This is the fulfilment I have searched for... this dream which I could never have dreamt without your help..."

He lost all control, rushed to her side, stretched out his hands to her.

"You are not to touch me, Matthieu," she said, "not yet. You will listen to me first, however great your impatience."

For the first time her speech had an undertone; she cleared her throat. "What you see, Matthieu, is make-up, nothing natural — something waxen, the mere form of the form — but without its colour or its intrinsic charm. People are different. I am different from what I seem. Franz, too, is different. You will scarcely encounter your accustomed reality in this town; sometimes perhaps as a strange, aberrant exception — or maybe not at all. For a while you will be deceived; then you will receive the blow that renders you senseless; this is that moment."

She clapped her hands as before. Once again the groom, Donkey, her little brother or whoever he might be, appeared at the door.

"Come in, Franz," she said.

He walked over to her; she placed an arm around his hips.

"Did Mr Matthieu kiss you?" she asked.

"No," answered the groom.

"Did Mr Matthieu unbutton your litevka?" she asked.

"No," he answered.

"Then I shall do it so that this gentleman will stop being so stupid."

With her free hand she tore open the young man's grey uniform so forcefully that Matthieu thought that the buttons would fly off or the lad would fall over. She tugged at him as if at an unyielding object.

It seemed that Donkey wore no shirt.

Matthieu screamed out loud, shrank from the pair. The groom's body was black. Not dark, like that of an African, glistening violet or olive-green-brown, nor dusky as ebony, but black as soot, black and dull, a mass of matt coal in human form. Above the blackness of his chest was his pale head, his yellow hair — and Matthieu realised that the graceful image, and the pretty mouth, were painted, a fake. Its essence was as black as the void, a hole in gravity, existence without form.

"His lips are frozen quicksilver," said Elvira.

She covered the youth's naked chest, buttoned up the litevka, looked at Matthieu's appalled face. He had resolved to flee, but became enchanted anew by Elvira's image.

The groom's face, a moment before like a stiff replica in a waxworks, also resumed its lively engaging character. His half-open mouth smiled, awoke as from rigor mortis, came to resemble Elvira's.

"I cannot grasp such wickedness. I love human beings…" Matthieu's words were barely comprehensible. He approached the groom, wanted to touch his mouth; but did not dare.

"You are not familiar with reality; that hampers your mind. What could be easier to grasp than this? The zebra has black and white stripes, and there are ponies with black and white patches, as if their coat were a map with oceans and continents, but they are both horses in shape. We have the shape of people; but in our case a dream, a black curtain hangs before our selves. The great nocturnal fields are not astonished by whiteness and blackness. Those who lie in them, dead or twinned in copulation, are dark."

"I agree," Matthieu replied to Elvira's words, "I see the fields with the dead thereon, and those overflowing, and the naked earth and the earth covered in grass... and that they are not present because they have been removed, taken away, destroyed." He no longer thought of flight. Elvira removed her arm from the groom. He left without speaking.

"Please, Elvira, please allow me to kiss you," Matthieu implored.

She pursed her lips and said dispassionately, without a trace of kindness: "I shall not refuse; but I prefer to avoid fleeting contacts. That might sound frivolous to you. I have but little in the way of a soul — that is my only excuse."

Matthieu felt rejected. He searched for a conciliatory word; but his mind was too confused to find a suitable reply. He merely uttered the woman's name, and it was unclear what the sound conveyed: incomprehension, renunciation, or an excess of wild emotion.

Elvira continued: "You may leave this house whenever you wish; you have no obligations. Whoever feels offended has squandered his chances."

"Elvira — I have no reservations..."

"Please don't talk as if you were a stranger, Matthieu! In the end each person behaves as he has learned and as befits him. But time is not on our side; sooner or later we are bound to discover this with great certainty."

"You distrust me, Elvira — above all my reason."

"Your flesh is willing; your spirit sleeps. But even flesh can be afraid. Right now you love my breasts. I have no doubt about that…"

She turned to the hidden door.

"I must take off my make-up and attend to a few things. I shall have Franz inform you when I am ready."

She disappeared. Not even her scent remained. Matthieu was dismayed, but also filled with inexpressible hope. His strongest emotion was not one of longing, but the certainty that no desire could match up to its fulfilment. At the same time he was unsettled by a strange emptiness in his mind. His thoughts were like fragments of thoughts, rather than a recognisable amalgamation of sensible ideas. Wherever they led seemed already extinguished — and every intention concerned with a distant future vanished. Even the sensation of impatient waiting dissipated into aimless acceptance. The groom — his figure scurried briefly through Matthieu's mind — had no more meaning, no purpose in Matthieu's reality. He saw the youth, inasmuch as one can speak of inner sight, as a light figure floating away at an angle into the distance — like an oversized children's balloon — his livery, neither solid nor transparent, but a grey shadow.

He was annoyed to find himself counting, his mind counting, and that the numbers produced a kind of hollow sound. Even Elvira… He stared at the hidden door, tried to reconstruct the image which had disappeared behind it. It remained incomplete in the midst of this unbreakable chain of numbers. Finally he sensed only a dark protest, an extreme demand from the life enclosed within him. The sum of the numbers and of his being transformed into a naked fixity of the will, as if he were a madman who gloated over one single impulse and expanded it into a universe.

He was alone. That sublime male form which he had grasped with forcible clarity a while ago, was gone. He no longer thought of it, no longer recalled the kindly warmth of the second body which had accepted his. He did not think of his own, more substantial being, which had been linked in a legitimate way with the other, whoever it might have been.

He had been cast here — into this new, unfamiliar longing — on the basis of a hunch. He called out to no one. He knew no names. He called out no names.

There was a knock at the door. The groom, Donkey, entered. His face was cool, without ambiguity, but still a puzzle, for in this nocturnal air it was but a breath of paper-thin make-up. "Green, like gold leaf held up to the sun. But I cannot see anything real behind it." Such were Matthieu's feelings.

Donkey sidled up to him and said: "Elvira awaits you, sir."

"Yes," he answered quickly, turning his eyes from the groom to the hidden door. Donkey walked to the door and opened it. He extended an arm invitingly to Matthieu. He stirred, hurried, heard that he must climb several steps inside the wall, went up, stood before a second door, noted that the hidden door must have closed, for it had become totally dark.

He gave a knock, listened, heard nothing. Knocked again, received no summons to enter. But he entered. At first he saw himself, approaching himself, closing a door behind him. Then he understood the perfect symmetry of the room: a room split down the middle and then extended

107

in imaginary fashion to create a whole. The wall in front of him was of glass — a single mirror which reproduced the objects and events. So Matthieu first saw the alcove, behind the glass wall as if it were in another world, which could not be entered, in irreality. As he walked towards it, he, his second self, moved away from his objective.

For a moment Matthieu was confused. Then he stood next to the enormous pane of glass, facing himself, close enough to touch, but unable to do so, studied himself, sounded the glass with his knuckles. "That's me," he said, "or at least I seem to be."

At once he recalled a memory, if very briefly, like the jolting sensation that awakens one when a sudden slackening of the pulse destroys a deep slumber and the only evidence that remains of the threat is an anxious uncertainty. "Here on this reflecting surface I am thinner than tissue paper. The angels have no tie racks in their cupboards on which to keep us as neatly folded cut-out figures, assuming we are their playthings — because they are naked. But they have mirrors. They press us into them, thin as a thought between two pages of a book — in so far as anything remains of us. GARI — not to become tissue paper — in our transformation we are not even as thick as tissue paper. Thousands upon thousands of shadows are stored within a single mirror, in every conceivable form — even our own — provided they have touched us once more than is agreeable to them."

It was as if another had spoken. The name had been found. The mirror had released the name, but not the form belonging to it. Matthieu looked for the second shadow, the shadow outside of him. He drummed harder on the glass. The moment had passed. The name had been named. And was forgotten again because the form disappeared.

Matthieu turned from this world he could never enter, walked to the alcove — the real one, not its mirror image — a recess in the wall, quite broad and deep. The bed inside it was covered in a bright red, one might even say dark pink velvet with shiny silken pillows and blankets of the same colour. Matthieu did not, however, see Elvira, as he had expected, but merely a swelling of the covers which indicated a prostrate person beneath.

"She's still hiding herself," he thought, then walked to the edge of the bed and said out loud: "Elvira, it's me."

"It's me, too," came the muffled reply.

He sat down on a stool beside the bed and studied the motionless form, full of unspeakable anticipation, but almost paralysed by shyness.

He wanted to say more, but every word seemed worthless. He waited for a movement — for a surprise, such as his existence had yet to be granted — for the eruption of a boundless emotion — a tremendous prelude and an intoxication at the same time— for perfume, feelings, a swoon and painless contact — for the greatest possible extension of his being.

Eventually this waiting seemed pointless, and soon even vapid. He felt that Elvira was not even there wrapped up beside him. His expectations were fleeing. Simultaneously he felt compelled to refute this threatening turn in his feelings of happiness, to refuse to renounce this moment for a lesser one. He grasped the cover and removed it with one brisk motion.

He saw Elvira. He had expected her to be naked. And she was. But she resembled the groom, Donkey, her brother — or whoever he might be —

in her blackness. A blackness with neither sheen nor shadow, that conveyed nothing, not even the shape of her body. For a couple of seconds Matthieu felt he was staring into a hole, or was behind the mirror, faced with a shadow with no origin.

Only gradually did his eyes come to terms with this bodily matter, like charcoal. He noticed a reddish, painted shimmer to her lips, a red amidst grey and green, like a glow among the ashes — and the same trace of dusty life around the loin-warm area of her thighs — a distant, abstract image produced by a daring mind. Matthieu could no longer imagine touching this figure — no longer and never again. His anticipated joy was followed by emptiness; only astonishment, an icy detachment remained; not even disappointment.

He attempted to verify what had happened. He bent his upper body over her, studied the breasts and saw that they were modelled on Elvira's, but transposed into blackness, devoid of flesh, of sensuality, as if made of fissured, expressionless pumice stone.

"Elvira... I am Matthieu..." he said at last to the closed eyelids in order to elicit a movement from the motionless body.

"The queen received her paramours in a bed of black velvet, for she had an exceptionally white skin. I am obliged to choose a different colour."

Now she stirred, lithe as an animal, stretched out her hands to him, threw herself at him, filled the black space of her body with the magnificence of the living. This void of colour became comprehensible — an incisive promise. Elvira's eyes remained closed.

Matthieu, who had edged away, approached the figure once more as it unveiled itself with the force of desire. He knelt beside the bed, in accord with Elvira and himself. Reality was twofold flesh.

"All of my feelings are strangely underdeveloped," he said. "Only with difficulty do I manage to make contact with the present. But now when I stretch out my hands up close to you, the moment will come, this moment. I love your blackness — love you in your blackness."

Then she opened her eyes. They gazed at one another. For Matthieu it was like being blinded without pain. He could not make out whether Elvira's eyes were as black as caverns or had any colour at all. He was looking into what had never existed, never been conceived, never come into being, something which remained motionless beyond form and matter, joy and sadness.

"No," he said, resolutely, withdrawing his extended hands, "not yet." And he rose from his knees. He no longer saw Elvira. He only heard her voice. A summons. She summoned the groom. He appeared. Matthieu saw him reflected in the large mirror, entering through a door which he had not noticed previously.

Elvira's voice was weak but clear. "Give Mr Matthieu his 50 francs back. He does not like me…"

Matthieu replied to the groom's face: "I didn't give you 50 francs, I haven't given anyone 50 francs. It's a mistake."

"Give it back to him, Donkey," said Elvira's voice. "He paid it to you. He needs it. He is poor. He has nothing apart from those 50 francs."

"That's not true. It's a mistake. The groom did not ask me for any money. Nor did I give him anything of my own free will."

"Accompany him outside, Donkey, to the back alley. The main gate is locked. Don't listen to what he tells you! Do as I say!"

"It's not true," said Matthieu.

But he was already moving towards the door. He left the room. The groom was at his side at once.

"Why is this happening?" Matthieu asked.

"You did not kiss me, sir. You did not unbutton my litevka…"

"And if I were to do so now, now that I have learned a few things — and neglected even more…?"

"You may do so, sir. But it will not change anything. You cannot go back."

Matthieu felt the need to cry. But the tears did not come.

"And if I did so, Donkey? I suspect you are not as strict as Elvira."

"For me each person is as pleasant as the next. But you won't go back. You cannot. You will no longer find Elvira."

Matthieu stopped. The groom used the moment to press a 50-franc note into the guest's limp hand.

"No," said Matthieu, "I didn't give you any money."

"You will need the money," answered the groom. "You are mistaken about your situation. Your pockets are empty."

Matthieu felt his clothes. He placed the note in the side pocket of his suit.

"Why are you so friendly, Donkey?" Matthieu asked. "I haven't given you a tip, I wasn't good to you…"

"Because you are lonely, sir."

"What do you know about me?"

"I know nothing, nothing about you, sir; but the hours have their attributes; they determine our behaviour..."

"Is it now the hour of blackness?"

"It is not that, sir."

"The hour was already here."

"It was not yet here, sir."

Matthieu lowered his head to hide his face. He thought of the change in Elvira's eyes, of the ungazing emptiness. It horrified him. Then he kissed the groom. He did not find that the lips were cool and had the stale taste of unbrushed teeth. He rested his head on Donkey's shoulder, embraced his neck. The sluice-gates opened inside him; a river of tears flowed from his eyes; and a sob racked him like a fever chill. He did not know what he was crying about; but he found it so easy to yield totally to a pain which seemed to have no deeper origin. Once the overpowering emotion was quelled inside him and his tears had subsided, he heard the groom speak.

"We mustn't remain here. We must carry on."

"Yes," said Matthieu. He released himself from Donkey and attempted to establish where he was.

They were standing in a grimy, dimly lit corridor, long with cracked stone tiles, windowless, with a far-away door which they now approached.

The groom walked arm in arm with Matthieu, like a friend. Matthieu stopped again.

"I do not want to go," he said.

"Every will is short-lived. Every wish fades," answered the groom, then tugged on Matthieu's arm.

They reached the door, entered a courtyard surrounded by a number of hushed buildings. A gateway led to a second courtyard, clearly similar to the first. And then a third courtyard. After they had crossed this, Matthieu made out four figures standing in a circle to one side of the path, beside the passage to the third gateway. He looked at the standing group. He felt he could distinguish enough of them to sense their outermost nature. A boy, fifteen or sixteen years old, strapping, strong, a dark shadow on his upper lip. A girl, fourteen or fifteen years old, buxom, strong, an unconscious life scattered over her entire body. Two smaller boys, fourteen or fifteen years old, more delicate than the first, watchful skins, strong wishes, but completely wrapped up in themselves.

"They desire one another; but speak trifling words," thought Matthieu. The group scattered as soon as he and the groom approached. The four figures leaned against the walls, made themselves motionless as mummies, prepared coarse remarks in case they were addressed by these strangers. Matthieu passed in silence, led by the groom.

"Who are they?" asked Matthieu after twenty or thirty paces.

"I do not know them, sir. They are my age; but I do not know them."

"Why are they awake, Donkey? It has been declared that the town should sleep."

"It is their life, sir. Their life is such that they stand and stay awake."

"Not everyone sleeps. I already knew as much," said Matthieu. They came to a standstill. The groom removed his arm from his companion.

"This is the street," said Donkey. "Your way, sir, lies straight before you."

"Is there a way for me?"

"I presume so," answered the groom.

Matthieu fell silent for a moment, searched for a question he wished to pose. When he turned his mouth towards the groom's face, he was no longer there.

"I have no will here that does not immediately melt away."

He noted a feeling of discomfort, like after mindless debauchery.

"I have not left anything of myself in any of these encounters. I have not forfeited anything..."

He walked in the direction the groom had indicated, not tired, but disheartened. With each step his memory of Elvira weakened, of the black delight he had missed, of his unfinished adventure, of Elvira's sweet brother who concealed a black, unsmoothed chest beneath a grey uniform. Matthieu retained virtually none of this. A black button — that was the last thing — a button, matt as cloth. A nipple of charcoal, Elvira's or Donkey's.

His eyes remained dry.

"It's getting cold," he said, and strode onwards. He scarcely recognised the course of the street any more. He paid no attention to the houses. The almost complete absence of light blurred everything — not mysterious, but deadened. The rubbish in front of the houses — dustbins or cardboard boxes filled with waste and refuse, with a uniform smell of staleness and extinguished fire, or acrid from unappetising matter — revealed that he was in an insalubrious suburb, or at least a side street, inhabited by people who scraped a living, or had gone to rack and ruin, soured by misfortune, nasty fumes and foul habits. Adults with no hope, in tepid beds, full of uncaring lust. Children cast from warm protection on to the floor so that they may crawl on it, foul it and eat from it. Youths full of precocious seed, prey to every disillusion, still illuminated by a strange assurance that some act of prostration or surrender will bring them bread and shelter. And workers, the wretched and laden — ceaselessly at their machines or in the uncounted rooms of the offices — whose start each morning has the punctuality of a church clock.

"Why is that so?" asked Matthieu.

And he answered himself: "Life become flesh has but one dictate: to exist and to continue to exist. Work fills the belly, if barely. Fornication fills the belly, if barely. He who eats dirt dies or resists. Existence is meagre; but it is a possession, so long as it lasts. It is also present in black skin and in festering flesh; behind blind eyes and in those with no testicles. Only later, when the warmed ferment has grown cold and sullied some spot…"

He knocked into a crooked object, stepped in filth, then stopped before a house in the belief that he could make out the letters of a sign. He read: *Barbara Fleissig, Midwife.*

"What difference is there between the unborn and the once-existent? Between the unformed and the once—created? The thought, the image is a trifle. Love, the bloodiest feeling — can it perish as if it had never existed? Can some memory of it outlive us?"

He wandered further. The number of signs he could have made out increased. But his indifference exceeded his curiosity.

"This suburb will come to an end," he thought.

But its extension was inordinate. He did not reach the end.

A person he had passed but not noticed spoke to him from behind. It was a young voice, not unlike the groom's, but less vibrant.

"Can you spare me a cigarette?" the voice asked quietly.

Matthieu stopped, felt in his pocket, turned to the speaker.

"I don't have any cigarettes on me," he answered.

The figure came closer, walking with difficulty or shuffling, so it seemed to Matthieu.

"That's really bad," said the approaching figure, "I thirst for a smoke. I haven't had a cigarette between my lips for ages."

Matthieu tried to make out what sort of person this was. "A young person," he determined, "obviously lame or with an infirmity."

"I don't have any cigarettes on me," he repeated, as if the other hadn't answered him.

"Do you want to accompany me for a while?" asked the other.

Matthieu hesitated before answering, tried to scent what was behind the question. Then he took a few steps away from the other. But the latter called out at once, urgently: "You must take me with you, sir! I am hungry. I have no bed. I am tired."

Matthieu answered: "I am a stranger in this town. I have no home here."

"There are hotels," said the other.

"The hotels are shut," said Matthieu.

The other wailed: "People without compassion should be long since asleep."

"Are you perhaps white?" asked Matthieu.

"If there was a light you would see who I am, sir," said the other.

"Is there a light anywhere?"

"Perhaps," said the other, and once again he was at Matthieu's side.

"If you know where I can find light we'll be fellow travellers. If there is an inn nearby which is still open you may eat your fill." Matthieu felt the bank-note in his pocket.

"I'm freezing," said the other.

"It has got colder," replied Matthieu.

He tried to hurry on, but his companion held him back. Yes, the other had grasped Matthieu's jacket and was letting himself be pulled along, so that they made heavy progress.

"We are making poor headway," Matthieu observed, "put your arm in mine if we are to be companions."

The other did so, and at once he was able to walk really well. He leaned on him slightly for support. Matthieu, weakened, felt the weight of the other's body, and at the same time a growing intimacy with the alien figure, of which he had guessed no more than his youth, his male sex; and that an infirmity, be it serious or otherwise, hampered the litheness of his movements: an ingrown toe-nail, a pain in the hip or irregularity of the bone structure; or even less seriously, a heel sore from walking, or flabby, adolescent muscles. But the two were making good progress, so Matthieu dismissed the possibility of a serious ailment. He convinced himself that it must be the toe-nail or growth pains.

They turned a corner. Having previously dragged his feet, the young man now led the pair. After stepping up and down the kerb several times, he stopped before a dark wall in which Matthieu recognised with difficulty a rudely fashioned door.

"Here's the entrance," said his companion.

"You go first!"

The other tried the handle. The door opened. The light scarcely increased. All the same, a narrow lobby could be made out. To the left a door opened of its own accord — or so it seemed. Stale warmth poured out from inside, the smell of beer, rank tobacco fumes and light. Real light which made things discernible.

"That's a comfort," said Matthieu.

He pushed in front and entered the restaurant first. It was quite unusual, for customers with a few small coins in their pockets. Not at all splendid. Tables, wooden chairs, long benches against the walls. At the back a bar of uncommon length and height, piled up with bottles. Beer taps twisted up from the thick mahogany top. A vitrine for food, metallic and sparkling. The shelves on the wall behind this construction contained drinking vessels in many shapes and sizes, and more bottles bearing various labels.

A barmaid — buxom, with a fat, waxen face, tired, painted eyes, bare arms, wearing a dress of drab red material — stood bent over the counter writing in a book. Evidently she was doing the accounts, because she was silently moving her mouth, as if her lips would enhance her memory of the numbers. She did not observe the new customers, did not even look up as they approached and sat down to one side of the counter on a bench against the wall. She carried on whispering numbers to herself, jotting down this or that result of her calculations with a thick blunt pencil.

Matthieu was very thankful that for a while he could sit as it were alone with his companion, unobserved. He even changed place, sat to one side on a chair, so that he could look the other straight in the face. He now had his back to the counter.

He studied this other person, made a conscientious examination which grew slower and slower. A person is a person, a second person apart from oneself. A male person has a male constitution. So one knows one another's feelings in advance, especially because a difference of scarcely ten years does not make for significant differences, or any strong aversions.

Their kinship or brotherhood did not appear this time to be of the general kind. The other's clothing had already prompted Matthieu to recognise something, something familiar in the other's appearance. A jacket of good cloth, pleasing both in cut and colour — as if he had chosen it himself — or had lent the other man something of his own. To Matthieu's astonishment though this jacket had clearly been rent with force and then carefully stitched together again. The seams were cobbled, their cross-stitches clearly visible. He stilled himself; he waited for a memory. It had not yet revealed itself; but it must already have hurried up close from the past. He stared at the other face, strangely perplexed, touched it, with his gaze, at first tentatively, then resolutely. He grasped the other's head with his hands, turned it to one side and then back again, touched the ears.

His emotions constantly welled up during this unseemly examination, which he repeated stubbornly, insistently, anarchically. His eyes wandered along the wall opposite in order to quell his confusion. Matthieu looked at the mirror hanging there, a magnificent brewery advertisement praising the excellence of its beer with letters etched in glass. Between the lettering at the top and bottom he saw two heads, his own and the other's. He not only recognised the image of his own face, but also the image of the youth as something that corresponded to himself. He tried to account for this to himself as quickly as possible. He looked back across a decade of his past and established that once, some time around the onset of adulthood, he had looked frequently at that face, every day, as something belonging to him, as his property, as the outer form of his being.

"It resembles mine," he whispered to himself, "that's how I looked eight or nine years ago, when I was fifteen or sixteen."

He established this without aversion, without reservation.

"It is my mirror image from back then," he continued to himself, "it has been preserved. But because it is some lovely thing that is worth repeating? Or because it so inconsequential that no one wanted the bother of altering it?"

He also realised that the youth was rather slight and seemed weighed down by sorrow.

Matthieu was beset by pain, turmoil, absurdity. He grabbed the youth, pulled him up close to the mirror, brought his head so close to the other that they touched, pointed to the reflection in the obliging glass.

"Do you understand that I was once the person that you are now? Can you see how similar we are?"

"The eyes, the hair..." the younger man stuttered, "but some things are different."

"Yes, yes," Matthieu sighed, "I have changed. My mouth is not so fresh, my cheeks are slightly plumper and greyer, from within, than yours. But I know that my appearance derives from the face that you have now — that you are something I have been. I can remember the image of my former appearance. A picture of sad grace, customary expectation or longing, indecision about life, this early attempt to be, to find sorrow agreeable, to throw oneself at a tenuous emotion — all the ineptness that is excused by youth..."

"I do not know how I shall look in ten years' time, if I live. The similarity between us will never be quite congruent."

Matthieu gave a harsh laugh. "We go to bed with our own self in the evening, but in the morning we see someone else in the mirror."

They returned to their places. Matthieu felt as if someone had exhausted his brain. All that was left in him was an anarchic roar. He sought vainly for connections, certainties, precise thought, for purpose.

"This is an encounter," he reassured himself at last, "an accident, a meeting, calculated, decreed — or unpremeditated, cast here, a superfluous occurrence, a waste product of the possible, unworthy of consideration..."

He said out loud: "Place your hands on the table!"

The other obeyed, spread out his hands before the older man. The latter placed his own beside them.

"Can you see it at last?" he asked.

The younger man remained silent.

"They resemble mine, a few years younger, not yet fully grown." Matthieu continued talking to himself: "They are my hands from former times. This is an untoward coincidence, because this person cannot be running around after me eight years later like my shadow incarnate. I had no seed that early on, and nor was there any girl." He shook his head with ill-humour and asked tersely:

"What's your name?"

"Matthieu," said the other.

"Matthieu? That's my name too. Twice the same, the same name, I don't understand..."

"Then please call me Other."

"Other? What do you mean? By what name?"

"Other resembles a name," said the youth.

"Other? Quite right. Other, Arthur. I'm slower on the uptake than you. Other, your name is Other. You are playing with me; but you're doing it well."

Once again he brought his head up close to the youth's.

"If you are made of the same stuff as I, and you're poor too, hungry, and cold; have no comfort, no home, no bed, nothing, just yourself, and your youth, which still has some value... Then things are bad for you; and you have a disreputable profession..."

The youth shook his head sadly. "I understand what you are implying," he answered quietly, "but I have yet to go with anyone. You are the first..."

"You're lying," said Matthieu.

"Only half an hour ago, as I spoke to you, did I first fall by the wayside.

Before then I was different. I had no resolve, didn't even know that one could resolve to do something. I have never smoked a cigarette. I asked you for one because that was my first ever decision. I justified it to myself because I didn't have a coin to my name."

"Don't you have any parents?"

"No," answered the youth.

"No one who finds you pleasing, who would be ready to help you?"

"Only one who likes me when he sees my blood flow. He wounds me, and worse with each passing day."

"You're lying…"

"He wants to dismember me, to take me apart like a clock. Until now I thought he had the right, that there could be no protesting. I remained silent. Just whimpered. I had no will. Today he looked deep inside me — through a yawning gash…"

"It is your right to lie," said Matthieu, "the lie is your protection, the handmaiden who praises you or makes you pitiable. I, however, have sought refuge until now in what truth and sincerity I could attain… They are no protection, as one discovers, but place us at the mercy of others."

"Is your skin everywhere intact? Have you never been cast to the ground and slit open?" asked the younger Matthieu.

"Yes," the older uttered painfully, "it can happen — it happens — it happened to me. But why do you have the same destiny?" The memory, held off afar like a menacing sea by dykes, lost its distance, roared up, rose up right to his soul. He saw images again that threatened to send him reeling. He was gripped by fear of what had been. "It has not passed away.

It is unchanged within me, it stands beside me, rejuvenated. A second I which suffers, even though my flesh does not feel the pain, another flesh submits to the pain instead." He whispered these words, inaudible to the other.

"Where then is the lie?" asked the youth. "Aren't I exposed now because I was honest?"

"Are you of the black or the white?" asked Matthieu, quite emptied by fear.

"Shall I lie, or tell the truth? Whatever I answer, it resolves nothing."

"Are you a stranger here like me, one who has just arrived, or an inhabitant?"

"I stood on the street and waited for a person who resembled me."

Matthieu was beside himself. The past seeped away once more, receded like ebbing water. He forgot where he was with the other. He drew the youth closer to himself, unbuttoned his jacket, hastily but less violently than Elvira had done with Donkey. Other also wore no shirt. His chest lay pale, shimmering before Matthieu's gaze, tender and decorated with two small pink circular patches. The youth leaned his head back so that his neck extended upwards, straight, almost white, from his body — so as to prove once and for all the veracity of his pallor.

"Was that once me?" Matthieu asked himself, "so slight and lean in build, so gracefully smooth, with soft muscles, not repulsive, pleasing in an average way, a person who can be taken or even loved, when one takes an honest look at him?"

He closed the youth's jacket. He remembered the barmaid; but it did not matter to him whether she had observed his behaviour or not. He saw that she was still writing and adding up. He turned back to Other.

"Is it useful or damaging for us to know that we are both the same pale colour — younger Matthieu, Other? But what an idiot I am! You don't know that about me!"

"Of course I know," answered Other, "because I don't doubt it."

"Ideas come quicker to you, for you have had to put up with much and ward off even more. I, on the other hand, brought up in the uncertain protection of another's care, have a hesitant mind, numb thoughts, a vacillating demeanour — no strength in love and only vague dislikes…"

"I am hungry," said Other.

Matthieu leapt up at once and went over to the counter. The barmaid had just closed her book, so she could now turn her attention to her customers. "What can I do for you, sir?" she asked.

"Something to eat, please, fortifying and plentiful…"

Mechanically the barmaid picked up a menu card, from in front of her, glanced at it, put it back and replied:

"There's nothing left to eat, sir."

Matthieu interpreted her refusal. "Nothing roast or boiled, but there must be bread, sausage, ham, cheese, pickled eggs, cold cutlets…"

"There's nothing left to eat," the barmaid insisted.

"Do you mean that the inn is about to close?" asked Matthieu.

"The inn will remain open, sir; but there is nothing more to eat."

"But you must be able to find a bit of bread, butter, some salad, a piece of meat — if you are willing — for a good price. The young man over there is hungry. He must have something to fill his belly. If the inn is in fact open."

"There's no meat left, sir."

"Then at least a slice of bread, a piece of cheese," Matthieu begged. "If you would just look. Just something. A plate of soup, perhaps..."

"There is no more bread left, sir. Yesterday's bread has been eaten. There is no more soup. It's all been eaten. There is no vinegar or oil. It has all been used up, for the night is already very long. As you can tell; all the customers have left."

"I don't see the connection."

"Everything is connected," replied the barmaid.

Matthieu returned to Other, despondent.

"There is nothing here to eat," he told him, "perhaps you could try to favour your stomach with a glass of egg nog. A large glass would warm and strengthen you."

Other nodded in agreement. Matthieu ordered the drink.

"We have no more egg nog, sir."

"But there's a bottle on the shelf! I recognise it..."

"It's empty, sir — empty to the last drop."

The barmaid took the bottle, uncorked it, held it neck down.

"As you can see, sir."

"The next bottle! Please. Or the next."

Patiently the barmaid fetched two more bottles, uncorked them and held them upside down.

"They are empty. I sell what I have. What I don't have I can't sell."

"Then give me two glasses of port, please," said Matthieu, dispirited, without asking Other whether he liked it.

"I can't help you with that either, sir, the bottles are empty."

"Don't you have any stocks in the cellar?" asked Matthieu.

"The bottles in the cellar are empty, have been since the onset of night."

"I don't understand."

"I'm telling it the way it is. You must come to terms with it."

"Then give us what you have in stock," said Matthieu.

"I have no stocks left, sir."

"So all these bottles are useless then?" asked Matthieu, incredulously.

"They are empty. Please confirm it for yourself, sir."

The barmaid now uncorked one bottle after another, held each upside down, replaced it.

"I've never seen anything like this," Matthieu said bitterly, "pour us a beer then!"

The barmaid turned one beer tap after another; but no liquid emerged.

"As you see, the barrels are empty," said the barmaid.

"I don't understand," Matthieu objected once more, "didn't anyone order supplies?"

"Of course, sir, we had plenty of supplies. But the night has grown very long, and at some point even the largest stock is exhausted."

"Was there an unusual rush of customers today?"

"Quite average, sir. But the night is longer than usual. As you yourself must know."

"I am a stranger here," said Matthieu.

"I have no answer to that," said the barmaid.

The conversation seemed to have come to an end. Matthieu returned to the table where Other was sitting.

"I have not achieved a thing," said the older man, "there is neither food nor drink." He turned back to the barmaid and spoke out loud:

"There must at least be a glass of water! A glass of water please!"

"I shall try, sir," answered the barmaid.

She went to the sink, turned the water tap. A thin trickle emerged and slowly filled the glass she held below.

"That will be the last of the water," she said, "you may have it with pleasure."

Matthieu walked up to the counter.

"That is strange. Why has the water dried up in the pipes?"

"It is an old superstition that the municipal supplies can be tapped for ever without being exhausted. It has turned out to be a false belief."

"Why do you stay open when you cannot even serve your customers a glass of water?"

"We have our regulations, sir."

"And when the regulations make no sense? When they no longer relate to any kind of reality...? To all appearances this is a tap room; but it is exhausted, rendered barren by over-use; the last glass of water has been handed out!"

"We don't let ourselves be misled by such objections, sir. We are duty-bound to keep this inn open until dawn. And should dawn never arrive, we shall never close."

Matthieu shook his head indignantly at so much nonsense. He tried asking the barmaid another question:

"Don't you even close the door when the last customer has left and no one else comes in?"

"Our regulations do not allow for that."

Matthieu thought for a moment. Then he spoke placatingly:

"It might appear that tonight's events gave a pretext for our conversation, but our words are simply an exaggeration. The earth has not disappeared into some chasm, or shifted its poles."

"I cannot answer that, sir; I only understand simple matters." The barmaid seemed to wish to end the conversation once and for all, but after a while Matthieu heard her continue:

"... In the depths of the night one knows nothing of the day. It is expected, but the time will come when we will never greet the dawn again. That at any rate is the general opinion in this town."

"Yes, okay..." Matthieu answered slowly, "but 'the time will come' is a vague expression which itself presupposes a long future."

"Or a short one," said the barmaid; "... all who believe in the patience of creation will be surprised by its violence."

"What do you mean by that?" asked Matthieu.

"One day the turbines which generate our light will come to a standstill, break down, or show their will in some other fashion. Water is also not in man's control, but part of a larger time than man."

"But we are not far removed from yesterday," answered Matthieu, "and yesterday there was still agreement between man and things. Water and machines do not become estranged from us that suddenly."

"I do not understand you, sir. Yesterday can be half an eternity away."

The barmaid picked up the menu and stared at it. From then on the conversation seemed to her utterly pointless, or exhausted. Matthieu remained at the counter for a while, perplexed. Then as he turned to the younger Matthieu, searching for words, the light began to flicker and its brightness diminished. When once it resumed emitting a steady light, it had lost more than half its intensity.

"The turbines are already failing," said the barmaid.

"Here is a glass of water, Other," said Matthieu, "it is the only one, the very last..."

"I am very thirsty," said the younger man, "do you mind, please, if I drink it all?"

"It is all for you," said Matthieu.

Then he recalled that Other had asked him for a cigarette. He bothered the barmaid once more. The cigarettes were also sold out, she said; but she was willing to give her guests one of her own private supply. Matthieu also bought a box of matches, and with this purchase regained some kind of optimism. At any rate, a failure would have embittered him, weakened him.

Once Other had smoked the cigarette, Matthieu suggested they leave and search for another inn. The young man was not particularly taken by this idea, even though he had repeated his complaints about hunger and thirst, while glumly smoking his cigarette. The longed-for inn would not be found. He also claimed that he did not know his way about sufficiently well to be of much help in the search.

Matthieu, less sceptical than his companion, dismissed these objections. They got up, bade farewell. As they reached the door the lights threatened to extinguish completely.

The two of them hurried outside.

But what a surprise! Some substance they could not immediately identify had mingled with the darkness: a grey, shimmering something that was not light, seemingly emitted by a substance that had not been present a little while ago. If possible, the sky was even darker than before; it was the ground that had changed. Matthieu stooped down to feel what it might be with his hand. He touched cold dust, a loose, icy deposit. It was snow. The realisation alarmed him greatly; he also felt a dust of snowflakes alight on his face and hands. He took a few steps on to the street; then without even asking Other, attempted to go back into the inn. The closed door no longer opened. Some mechanism or other had locked it, quite by chance, or had it been bolted by human hand?

"We must try our luck elsewhere," said Matthieu.

"The snow is thick," said the youth.

Matthieu noted that his companion's teeth were chattering.

"Take my coat, Other!"

The youth allowed Matthieu to take off his coat and to wrap him inside it.

They set off, not knowing which way they should go. But Other set a course. He had taken Matthieu's arm once more, pressed himself gently against him. The coat seemed to warm him, or at any rate he no longer trembled.

Since they had no definite goal, but simply hoped to come across an inn or hostel, they had the leisure to keep a watchful eye on the night. They strained their senses.

"It has got colder," said Matthieu, "we are being dusted with ice."

They stopped, examined the loose snow through which they were trudging, which rendered their steps silent.

"It is already up to our ankles," said the younger man.

The older stuck out his tongue, tasted the icy granules which were falling thicker and thicker, cloaking the last remnants of the visible like fog.

They strode on, silently side by side, filled with vague notions, like animals who experience the fierce onset of winter and merely sense that harsher times have begun: adversity.

They noticed that their clothes had become completely icy and covered in snow. It was already too late when they turned up the collars of their coats and jackets. Matthieu suffered from the cold, which became increasingly bitter by the moment. But the youth's susceptibility to it had awoken his compassion. So he froze while the younger one was granted a modicum of comfort, even if it was to be short-lived.

Gradually the air filled with noises, unless their sense of hearing had become so acute they could perceive the muffled sounds that surrounded them.

On stopping again, they could hear the gentle tinkling of the crystal stars, the sound of the tiny flakes of ice. An eerie song with a monotonous melody of just a few high-pitched notes which, conducted by an invisible wind, developed into a rhythmic, ever-varying crescendo and decrescendo.

An inexhaustible melody, glacial, lulling perhaps, which deadened the senses but held off real sleep by its undertone of ineluctable disaster — the freezing of all liquid.

"Rain has a different countenance," said Matthieu.

Other understood what the older man wanted to say. He answered:

"It sounds like parched grass by the sea, or like a window pane crashing while you're sleep."

The wind grew stronger. Its dark tones as it passed beneath the roof tiles, or through the invisible trees, continued to be muffled by the ever-thickening stardust. But the gently falling billows were now coalescing under the buffeting of the air, to be spun through space, pressed down, lifted once more, gathered into dunes. And the cold bit all the more.

Walking became ever more laborious for the two wanderers. Sometimes they stumbled. On one occasion Matthieu sank to his knees, into the soft cushion of a grey mound.

The youth pressed himself closer to Matthieu, squeezed his arm, jostled the older man's thighs with fleeting obtrusiveness.

Matthieu tried to forget the other's body, to not feel this contact, but the attempt had the opposite effect. The notion that he was walking beside himself as a younger Matthieu became more compelling. He almost acknowledged to himself that he was in love, in the other, with himself. Eventually he admitted that he loved the other more than himself; because the other was younger, not yet worn out by the uncertain future of the next eight or nine years.

Scarcely had he admitted this than he heard a half-suppressed sigh.

Other had yet again come to a standstill, bent double and whimpering quietly. Matthieu asked in vain what was the matter. He received no answer. They moved on, more slowly than before.

"Do you know where we are?" asked Matthieu. "Do you recognise the street? Do you know your way?"

"Yes," answered Other quietly.

The melody of the snow-storm became louder. Mixed with it was the sound of an organ descending from on high. Icy needles lashed their faces, and it seemed more and more as if their flesh was naked in the devastating breath of the cold.

Other could now only drag himself along. Matthieu could not see whether his young companion was limping again or whether he was simply stumbling from exhaustion. The young man spoke:

"I can't go on. I can't go on very much longer. We'll never make it to a hostel. You must leave me here beside the road, or carry me in your arms."

"I shall not leave you," Matthieu replied briefly.

After a while he sensed his rather surly assurance had been of little comfort.

"We must try and enter one of the buildings. What we need more than anything is shelter." He had to admit that he too was frozen to the marrow.

Other did not think it advisable to break in somewhere. He thought it quite impossible. All the doors were locked and bolted, he said. And worse still was the danger. It would be better to freeze to death than to be felled from behind, with skull split open.

Matthieu did not even attempt to counter this ill-timed speculation; he felt the same. He merely said:

"Then I shall carry you."

It was no easy matter holding the younger Matthieu in his arms and carrying him through the glassy, chiming drifts. Soon the older man was panting and could feel his limbs growing weaker, the nerves inside becoming numb.

"You're heavy," he said apologetically as he placed Other back on his legs, to catch his breath for a moment. "It will be easier for me if I carried you on my back, like a horse," he added.

Other attempted to clamber on to his shoulders; but his efforts were shy and awkward and he did not succeed. So Matthieu bent down, pushed his head between the youth's thighs and straightened himself under his burden. He clasped Other's legs, and it seemed that he was seated comfortably. At any rate, after only a few steps they began a game. The younger man gripped the older's head, even grasped his mouth, forming a bridle with two bent fingers as if he were a horse — and set the direction by pulling his cheeks from inside.

"I cannot recognise anything any more," said Matthieu after playing the patient horse for a long time. His words were indistinct because he had Other's fingers between his lips and the oncoming wind produced a hollow whistle in his cheeks.

Matthieu noted that his face and hands were losing all feeling, that each step was becoming more arduous, that the snow almost reached his knees.

"We cannot carry on into the unknown," said the horse to the rider.

"Halt, steed!" cried Other.

Matthieu stopped because his mouth was being yanked apart by the finger bridle. Other appeared to be thinking or sleeping. Matthieu stood patiently in the snow because it made no difference whether he carried on or not. Finally the rider said:

"I didn't want to return to the cellar. But there is no mercy. I must return to it. If you were to accompany me, it might herald the onset of mercy."

"Which cellar are you talking about?"

"My home. It is terrible there. It is a place to die in. I did not want to die, but now I realise that I will just as certainly expire out here. Taking to the street has not helped. You have been friendly, Matthieu; but you have not put me in a warm bed. If now you would help me, so that I don't perish alone, abandoned by all the world, it would be a final consolation; if you would stay with me, just out of pity…"

Matthieu did not take in his words. All he heard was salvation. "A cellar is better than this icy night. Is it far from here?"

"No," answered Other, "we are on the way there."

"Right then, spur on your horse if you know the way! Can you see anything of the world? Is it still a scrap of dirty canvas?"

Other kicked Matthieu's sides with his toes.

"Giddy-up," he said, "a good horse doesn't get lost and can find its way through even the thickest of snow drifts."

Matthieu could make nothing out. He felt the fingers in his mouth and went on with eyes closed, simply obeying the signals that were given to him. He stopped now and then, sweating, but simultaneously gripped by icy hands. He felt he could no longer recall a thing. A blank void devoured the images in his mind along with any desires before they were even able to form. Even these pauses granted him no clarity. He did not know who it was on his back, why he was carrying him through the night. He had yielded himself up.

"Life, a young life is something precious, whatever cast it may take," he mumbled to himself. "The allure of youth... I am carrying the allure of youth." He did not know what the words in his mind meant. At any rate he did not dare put Other down. Nor did he attribute any meaning to this adventure. He contented himself with words that had no real import. He acknowledged his inability to continue this conversation with himself, but the desire to do so remained in him, even if with words that were nought but foolishness and heightened the equally complicit conceit of his aimlessness. He was like an animal beneath his rider in humiliating solitude.

The encounter had occurred. Was now irrevocable. He had been commanded to carry a person through the snow, to carry on until he had reached a goal he did not know — or a stop became necessary — until it proved impossible to carry on. Ultimately, even the most faithful horse throws itself down when the snow reaches its belly and it is incapable of raising its hoofs and moving on. It does not say it cannot go on, it simply falls to one side, exhausted like a person lost.

He trudged on, without confidence, yet not completely disheartened. Gradually his feelings for the rider disappeared completely. Matthieu was carrying a burden, a bundle, regardless of whether it possessed human warmth or was now just a weight, an accumulation of heaviness. He no longer felt the cold, but more that he was overcome by fatigue, as gigantic as boundless space, that robbed him of all his faculties. Suddenly he was cast out of this space. He felt the corners of his mouth being pulled apart. He stopped. He opened his eyes. He was standing in front of a wall, so close that he could have touched it with his forehead. The rider steered him sideways along the wall, clapped his thighs as a sign that Matthieu should release his arms and allow him to slip from his shoulders.

"Here we are," said Other, and he pushed open the door.

Matthieu placed his hands on the wall. It was a comfort to feel the stone, to gain the certainty that the town was still there. It had been displaced, but not dissolved. In a sudden blaze of terror he recalled the dark field which had been spoken of earlier that night; that had they been driven from the town it would have curdled his blood and his companion's, these two lost ones, stamped with exhaustion, unable to counter the ceaseless cold even with all of their bodily warmth. No, he did not think this, either with trepidation or with the force of a bold image, rather the taste of the idea, of the words, had come to his hands as they touched the cold wall. With this first clear thought he lauded the cellar, which he had not yet seen, and Other's faculties, for being able to find his way here.

"It is good that you bought matches," said the younger man, "the steps descend steeply, just after the door."

He asked Matthieu for them and struck the first directly after passing through.

Matthieu tried to shake the ice and snow from his jacket, stamped his feet, huffed warm air into his hands, and dusted Other down cursorily with a couple of brisk movements, clumsy from numbness.

They descended the steps by the light of the second match. The stairs were long, straight, enclosed by walls. As the feeble light of the flame died, they groped their way down in the darkness. Matthieu began to count the steps, regretted not having done so from the very start. When he counted the fortieth step, Other lit the third match so that his companion would not lose heart. They were still ten or twelve steps from the bottom. A long, vaulted passage became apparent.

On reaching the floor, Matthieu hesitated.

"We are deep underground," he said.

Other confirmed this.

Matthieu welcomed the warmth, this old exudation from the walls and the depths; but beside this blessing he also felt the sense of being enclosed bear down on him. He plucked up courage; he was afraid. The flare of the next match relieved the oppressive sensation, his curious misgivings. He eagerly allowed himself to be taken by the arm and led on.

"We can walk a while in the dark," said Other, "the passage is straight. There are no steps."

Matthieu wanted to say something, to intimate that he had an old compulsion to walk forwards in the dark. But his urge to convey this remained weak, indecisive, while at the same time he yielded to the bizarre images in the darkness, to the bright fireworks that flickered across the retinas of his eyes, distorted grimaces which, without any imagining on his part, rose up from unknown depths into the dawning of intentions that belong to no one, which form because blackness is the womb of all beginnings.

He gave a start as this was all pushed aside by the thought that this being beside him, who was leading him, whose existence he had come to know, was his own self, his second self, his younger self, whom he had once accepted and did so again — more certainly and more intensely even than before — as a better epoch of his flesh, a better part or a more valid state of his existence, so that his greater age became something disgraceful, an unexpected accusation that he could not ward off. He attempted to slip into his younger self, to extinguish himself and everything that he had felt or seen until this moment, so as to be only the other. He had been this way once; he scarcely doubted that; so something of what he had been might still reside within him, some substance or dimension, a retrograde motion, a reversal of time, an unspeakable wish.

The transformation for which he strove failed to materialise; the youth beside him remained a distinct individual, Other. Matthieu surfaced from his curious hankering to dissolve, to enter the other, and retained the certainty of that power of love that had already touched him in the tap room, but which now took possession of him like an eternity, shifting the bounds of his perceptions into the immeasurable. He savoured the fullness of being, once his own, now completely transposed to the other, and — disgusted with his inner uproar, with his powerful inner declaration of love — he simultaneously tasted the weariness, the hopelessness and the corruption of his available means for his attempt to combine two similar entities separated by two different times.

He felt he had come from afar, covered enormous distances, travelling on ships and trains — without being aware of his destination, on a ticket that had long since expired or had never been valid — in order to be perverted, changed — with a crazy result.

"I have come this far," he thought, "but my journey has been in vain. I shall not gain anything. All of a sudden I shall not know why or how I have ended up in this cellar — in the isolation of an unfamiliar building in an unknown town. I am walking beside a person who shortly before I did not know, and who I now believe — contrary to all reason — I know as well as my own self. Why does this being exist, this faltering life which opens itself up to me? Why have we found each other? We are but shadows to one another, interpretations that are incorrect, some straw or other, drifting in time…"

He stopped.

"Other," he said out loud, "would you help me please, help with all your heart; I am unable to comprehend this on my own — interpret our encounter, our mutual bond. I do not want to carry on as long as I am able to turn and leave. You are safe now from the cold and the snow-storm. We are in a cellar, which you say is your home. It is a poor home, but it is familiar to you — reluctantly familiar. What I mean is: you left this place tonight and have now returned. If I were to leave now, then not much will have changed for you. You will have lost a little time, meaningless time. Your hunger has not been sated; but that is not my fault. I can give you some money, so that you can buy food to eat, if there is food to be had. That is no more my affair than that you stood on the street and spoke to me. So we shall part our ways. I will return to the cold outside; that is my affair; I have decided and I alone bear the responsibility."

"There are various ways you can shake me off," replied Other, removing his arm from Matthieu, "but how will that help you? I would be deeply grieved, and you would be unable to forget that this was your doing. Behind a door, fifty paces farther on, I shall be lonely, at first — and then perish, fade swifter than a blossom that has been plucked and cast to the ground. And you will regret that you left me; for you cannot turn back the course of events, cannot repeat an encounter that can only occur once. Admittedly you were not looking for me; but you found me. And that's what counts. Money won't help me, as you know, for there is neither bread nor wine for sale, because another time has arrived. Everyone in this town is ready to give you money because it would be an empty promise. Yet no one will fill your belly. The grey nocturnal snow will not vanish so quickly. You too will sink into it from inordinate fatigue and no longer notice what nature inflicts on you. You will not find a welcoming house. You will not find another person who has a skin like you and me... So why do you want to leave me when there is no reason other than your stubbornness or your rebellion against the order of things which brought us together? The one whom you furtively seek, whose name you no longer know, whose form and being you have forgotten, who is less than a memory, this merest semblance of a longing — this drop of poison with no action: he is no longer by your side. I alone am still here with you."

Matthieu felt only the merciless blackness that enveloped him. The youth's voice came out of the darkness, seemingly from far away, immaterial. The older man was not beset by fear, but by a complete detachment from his senses, a dissolution of his bodily sensations. As if he were something that had trickled or seeped away, was no longer bound to, or at the mercy of anything. The sole dimension within and without him was the unrecognisable.

"I shall go with you," he said sombrely, "but before you take me by the hand again, please strike a match — so that we can recognise each other once again as something real..."

Other hesitated.

"We must be sparing with the light," he said after a pause, but then he struck a match.

"Sometimes one hesitates," Matthieu said to excuse his behaviour; "afterwards one is all the more resolute... We resist because we do not know ourselves, and even less so our neighbour."

The meagre flame was extinguished. Other took Matthieu once more by the arm and led him on. After several dozen steps he sensed they had entered a warmer section of the cellar tunnel. He stopped, checked his observation, remarked upon it.

"The effluents from the town are flowing beneath us," the young man answered, "it is the main sewer. The sullage is warm. It is an unappetising thought, but my abode is warmed by filth."

"Perhaps it is the warm water from the machines," Matthieu objected.

"It is the sewer," Other insisted.

After another twenty steps they felt the door.

But the door did not open easily. The youth used another match, and Matthieu saw that there was no lock in which to insert a key. It consisted of a couple of wooden boards which were distributed over a number of roughly hewn uprights, which Other pushed inwards in a particular order. As he moved the last the door swung open. Blackness returned at once, and in blackness the two of them crossed the threshold. Matthieu groped forwards for a couple of steps on his own, because his companion no longer led him. It was apparent that the door had closed again and Other was bolting it; or so Matthieu assumed from the sounds. He also heard the youth walk round the room, whose dimensions could be sensed from its own particular accumulation of hollow sounds; then move away, and finally stop in a corner and light the stump of a candle sticking out of a bottle. Matthieu watched this action. The cellar revealed itself to him in the glow of the light, which gradually grew bright and steady, and seemed for a few seconds normal, but then quite strange.

Other had said that this was his home. The only resemblance to a lodging was a chair, standing as if by chance at the centre of the room; and the lamp, in so far as the candle and bottle could be taken for one. There was no window. That was explicable by its location deep in the ground. Moreover Matthieu had not forgotten that there were houses in this town that lacked window openings, whether for some valid reason or not.

Despite the isolation and deep location of the cellar, the air was pleasant, unspent, without a trace of mustiness or staleness. Matthieu's eyes sought a vent, but discovered none. The room was medium sized, roughly six paces wide and eight paces long, and barrel-vaulted, its low ceiling everywhere within hand's reach. The paint on the walls and the ceiling was a uniform dusty distemper.

"You said that this is your home, Other. Don't you have a bed in which to sleep?"

Other pointed at the floor, but not to indicate that the brown lime flagstones were his resting place; he was drawing attention to an unevenness in the flooring, to an oblong wooden hatch which interrupted the regular rectangles of the stone slabs.

Matthieu made an ambiguous gesture and asked the still silent Other: "What is underneath?"

"Take a look!" came the answer. Matthieu walked to the hatch. Wooden boards, long but very narrow, were set in an oakwood frame; a trapdoor that could have led to the dusty coffins of a catacomb. Matthieu mastered this morbid, uncanny deviation in his thoughts, which hailed from a confused memory of an old village church.

"Is it a trap door?" he asked the youth.

"No, my bed."

"You sleep on the wooden boards?"

"No, underneath."

The terse exchange had already come to a standstill. Matthieu spotted a small oval iron ring affixed to the hatch, clearly to allow it to be opened.

"I must sit down," said Other.

Matthieu turned to him, helped him take off his coat, shook the water, melted snow, from the garment he had lent the youth, pulled over the chair. Other sat down gingerly, pulling a face. It was grey, sunken, angular, scored with pain. He emitted a dark moan, touched by the frost of his anxieties, and then he slumped as if in a stupor. Overcome, he accepted his condition without protest. At first Matthieu misinterpreted his placidity; it reassured him.

"I had quite forgotten that you are ailing," he said, his concern implying a request for more information.

"You already know," the youth stammered, putting an end to the other's curiosity for the moment. Henceforth Other experienced his pain as something damp, a sort of trickling away, with a sticky quality, monotonous, a hideous distortion of his bodily sensations, only just bearable; but he attempted to ward off any intrusion upon his miserable state. The incomprehensible emptiness in his head, a reeling sensation, a gentle disregard relieved him of its bleak, meaningless messages.

All of a sudden Matthieu thought he could feel the appalling isolation of the other, the nature, the details of his suffering. Yet still he hesitated to truly admit to himself what had flashed through his mind. His thoughts scurried back and forth in a zigzag.

"Why is the bed sunk into the floor?" he asked.

"Why are people placed beneath the grass when they no longer move and exhibit all manner of odious putrefaction?" the youth asked, pained.

"That is not what I wanted to think about right now," said Matthieu, "there are no parallels."

"Even crooked lines are aware that they could have been straight if some bungler hadn't done a shoddy job."

Matthieu did not respond to this easily contested expression of bitterness or despondency. Instead he returned to earlier in the conversation, and explained that he did not know the nature of the suffering that plagued Other.

The youth screwed his face into a distorted grin.

"Really?" he shouted. "You forget. You have undergone much the same — then, as well as later... All these stages of base affliction, of physical renunciation, of disfigurement, of disappointed expectations — and simultaneously a burning desire. If I am the return of yourself aged fifteen or sixteen, something preserved, your inner and outer likeness — of this former existence immured within you, key to your greatest experiences which have not dissolved like the sweet filth of the many days which have become a matter of indifference to you — if I am this shadow which has followed you from afar, lain in wait for you, finally to reveal itself — and now penetrated into you, once more become flesh and image — your best friend, your only friend, which was cast aside yet had permanence — then you know my wound!"

"Other... it seems impossible... this delusion... It cannot be. You have my face, my hands from then... as if the first seed on my fingers had found the womb; you have my age, which once I was, but which then I lost... a monstrous, bitter display of a useless, impure sweetness, that is what we find in each other... But not this wound, this wound once inflicted on me, in the meantime closed to a scar, this sign which has marked me, it cannot have been thrust upon your body in the identical manner in order to prove that we can become ugly! No!"

Matthieu had gasped and whispered by turn.

The youth sat up again, as if he had merely slept. His face looked as though behind a misted pane, almost effaced; it was an evil mist of a mouth that spoke:

"It is too late to turn back. All the doors are closed. All the streets are blocked. You have recognised who I am. You know that you have met your own self. There can be no more refuge in lies. You are in the midst of your confession. A knife was driven slowly into your belly. It left a red twisted scar…"

Matthieu began to scream.

"You see me in my nakedness, for you are describing my disfigurement. You know that I was cast down, to be slain. You know the reality which chose me as its stage. A gang of young conspirators gave entry through my skin to angels and demons. A total revolution occurred in my mind, a new awareness of being sweet mud, of being cast to the ground, bleeding — and then to recognise an angel, to which one becomes enslaved — entrusting in it with blind adoration. This alteration, bleeding, rent open, half murdered, with rapacious gaping spectres pouring into my entrails with seemingly interminable slippery scorn — inverting everything, thoughts and desires. No! You cannot have this wound! It is my fate, it was allotted to me. My callowness, the sap within which overwhelmed me, which delivered me up to such baseness, confounded me through its unnatural ignominy…"

He did not complete his sentence. In confused contemplation he studied himself like a stranger, dispassionately. He was weakened, as if from a substantial loss of blood.

"No," Matthieu repeated, "… the mirror might have deceived me. I would never have recognised you as a living human being, were you walking towards me. I recognised you only in the mirror, behind a deceptive pane of glass. It awoke my memory, for I often studied myself in the mirror, but it seems that the mirror lied. A mirror like that one in the inn, with a brewery's advertising slogan etched across it."

"We placed our hands next to one another," Other tried to object. "And why in fact shouldn't we be the same? Why shouldn't creation have conjured up such an accident? What difference is there between us? Flesh and bones are already repetitions *per se*, and thoughts and words our mutual playthings. We have eyes and lips in order to communicate, to strengthen our intertwined memories, and a masculine adornment whose inner will overpowers us. And so all that we have becomes undeniable: the same wound. Only a few years prevent us from merging into total sameness; one of us has been given too many, the other too few."

"That sounds as if there could be no lie in it; nevertheless… you see me in my nakedness, or rather, I am naked; which is already a falsification." Matthieu fell silent for a moment, and then continued: "Strange, I have already discovered tonight that I am unable to conceal myself, am no longer protected. But you have remained the other while in your clothes. You have not been excluded from the agreement."

Without a word of explanation Other began to undress. At first Matthieu did not grasp what the youth intended, but then his jacket lay on the floor, and his trousers were unbuttoned.

"No, I don't want you to do that!"

"I want to go to bed," Other explained simply, "it is necessary."

He wore no shirt. The jacket had been torn. His trousers gaped open at one thigh. And shortly the youth stood there with a rag covering his stomach and navel. And this rag was soaked in blood. A rag, grey in colour, bearing a congealed stain.

— —

Matthieu felt as if he had received a blow to the chest, then a second, more painful one; he could not have said where. He did not grasp who or what could have delivered these blows. At any rate his body shuddered to the roots of his veins. His knees buckled. But he knew that it was not his memory that had overpowered him; it had scarcely stirred. The convulsion more resembled a severe surgical operation, performed without anaesthetic or preparation. The sudden loss of an organ had become a certainty, a step in the process of self-eradication.

Immediately an overpowering compassion welled up inside him, an unutterable feeling of affection and a desire to help. Only with difficulty did he suppress a cry. Now he approached the youth.

"Other... how was I to know that you were suffering like that? You tore your shirt to cover the wound. I can't understand how you have managed to bear this painful abomination ever since we met, without revealing your injury..."

He dared not speak loud or fast. He took the youth by the shoulders, lifted him up tenderly, carried him back to the chair, lowered him gently.

"I was negligent. I should have pressed you when I noticed your difficulty in walking. I carried you for a while, to be sure; but I should have treated you more carefully."

Other stretched out his legs, and in a moment of boyish resolve tore off the sticky rag with one quick motion of the hand, emitting a kind of dark moan in the process. The saliva on his lips formed a couple of bubbles which burst. Then he said, calmly:

"Take the candle. Look at me closely! They have made a hole in me. I am open."

Matthieu remained, unresolved, where he was. The moan still echoed in his ear, as if it were the melody from a shell pressed to his cheek. Then he went over with the candle stump and illuminated the wound. It was not large; a slit with grimy edges; but the opening was deep and revealed at its bottom something pink and round, the minute part of a twisting inner tableau, something of the earthly substance or origins of this fifteen- or sixteen-year-old form.

Matthieu returned the bottle with the candle stump to its place in the corner. He wondered what he should say, what he should do. Other anticipated him.

"I am in a bad way. It would be senseless to look for a doctor. The doctors in this town are asleep; they are of the blackness. The snow, too, has blocked the streets, and the cold would freeze your lungs to stone."

"There must be some mercy," said Matthieu. "If I offered you my all, my love for you, all the thoughts of which my mind is capable, the water in my mouth to slake your thirst, the blood between my muscles to nourish you, my clothes to warm you — then surely some shred of mercy must enter from outside."

Other stretched himself slightly and looked at himself with unintentional, sad desire.

"How beautiful it would be were this filth not upon me! How pleasant it would be, the two of us! I would give everything…"

"Be quiet!"

"Without this disfigurement we would never have met. You would never have come to this town. People wish to dissipate us, the one by means of the other…"

"I do not wish to hear these confused thoughts," Matthieu hissed. His voice sounded hard. Bitter and over-zealous he had only heard the repugnant aspect of these words, not the ingenuous lament at the loss of a joy that had yet to have a name.

"Our life is one of confused events," the youth returned precociously, "confused words contain hidden wisdom."

Matthieu remained unbending. The waves of pity, irrepressible just a few minutes earlier, had dispersed. The venom of indifference had paralysed the core of his mind with inconceivable speed. He felt fatigue, exhaustion, emptiness. The sensation of having a human existence was as if swathed in mist. Vague, distant and detached, he saw himself being cast to the ground at some meaningless time beneath a grey sky in the concealment of leafless shrubbery, then roughly denuded, set upon and tormented by innocent, reprobate youths as if he were their enemy. One of them sliced his flesh, attempted to rip him apart with his fingers. He screamed before being gagged. Another, whom he did not know, an adolescent, a child-like angel, unrecognisable because he had no distinguishing feature, brought the slaughter to a halt. Another angel, brown, naked, with the muscles of a boy, not some solemn white guardian, but a guttersnipe, a bastard as it turned out, a young, inexperienced nobody who later dressed like the other louts — came to his assistance, prevented the mould from growing in his mouth before his time... And now this youth in the cellar had the same wound. Why the recurrence? Was there some meaning to the fact that he was left alive? That he had been assigned a nondescript angel, who understood less of existence than a reasonable human being? Who could do no better than to take him wandering for years on end through black fields, black streets, through black forests and black waters to a black town in order to reach the point where their wanderings began: a wounded Matthieu, fifteen years old, white-skinned but smeared with blood and disfigured for all time by a red scar across his smooth belly?

"It seems I now understand why the louts from the street wanted to murder me, and who it was that prevented them from doing away with me for good. So tell me how it was with you."

Other did not stop long to think.

"The people in this town are very average and lead a normal life filled with toil. They are easily satisfied, diligent and in love with order. They live for a couple of decades in their homes; then they are removed, disappear into the great black field which surrounds the town. Some are cast into the river. They all wear clothes because their bodies have a blackness black as coal. None will reveal whether this blackness increases their pleasure when they are naked. When one among them happens to be white and reaches a certain age which they consider to be the most pleasing, it incites their rage because they feel deceived, cheated. They do not slay the stranger at once; they have a means of death which works slowly. They wound the future outcast. At first they merely weaken him with small losses of blood. They apply the knife day after day. Gradually they cut deeper... With me it has reached the point where they have abandoned me, for my wound will no longer heal."

Matthieu listened to these words without any particular interest. They did not surprise him. He found nothing unusual in them. "Those are the laws that govern this town," he thought briefly, "people of coal, who sometimes wear white make-up, insist on their privileges." He asked then: "How, in what way, did you come to be here? Surely you were not born here of black parents?"

"How, in what way, did you find your way here?" the youth asked in turn.

Matthieu did not reply. It was too much effort to explain himself; his thoughts were unclear and full of curious gaps. He attempted to reach some understanding of his situation and self, but came up with nothing he could verify. To his own amazement he began to examine the sensations in his body. He observed that the trickle of spittle was absent in his mouth; there was no pressure on his bladder; his heart beat as regularly as the soft swing of a pendulum; he breathed as inconspicuously as in sleep. "I have no desires of any sort," he noted, "no urge compels me. My mind is like a swamp drying out under a motionless sky..."

The youth, lean, narrow-hipped, flat as a corpse, more like a grey plaster cast than a warm human being, had stretched out his legs so that a new gush of black blood trickled in a twisting line down his left flank. Matthieu saw this sign, like a black vein in pale stone. He asked for water, for a cup.

"There is no water, there is no cup," the youth replied.

"There must be some container, some possibility..."

"Open the hatch in the floor! It is high time!"

The older man obeyed. He grasped the ring, pulled, raised the lid which opened sideways and almost vertically, so as to remain open and leaning against the wall. Matthieu saw a long pit lined with brick, and fitting exactly inside, a narrow cot with pillows, sheets and blankets, almost snug... an unexpected contrast to the cold cellar. Admittedly the location was not only unusual, but also disconcerting; the resting place resembled a grave or coffin, if more comfortably appointed, slightly more spacious...

"Do you always sleep in this recess?" Matthieu asked, even though Other had indicated as much.

The youth nodded his head while righting himself on his chair, raising his arms and stretching.

In the same moment the wound opened up and some portion of his gut was extruded. He groaned, bent over double. Matthieu hurried over to him, took him in his arms.

"You must put me to bed."

"I can't see very well. I shall place the candle nearer. Prop yourself against the wall for a moment. Then I'll help you."

Matthieu carefully carried out his intentions. The candle now illuminated the cot in the pit. The older man knelt down, folded back the cover and then lowered the youth into the bed.

Matthieu stared helplessly at this picture of misery. He would have liked to place the covers over the pained figure at once, but the youth's state prevented him. It was impossible to turn from him in indifference. The gut had to be replaced in the body cavity. Matthieu sensed that he would be unable to stave off death; but though powerless, he would oppose it. In truth, he could not think of this death. He did not know what was to be lost or gained. His feeling of love, which had vanished so completely, now returned accompanied by an indefinable self-accusation, the reproach that in his initial dull confusion, he had recoiled and not really heeded the other's cry for help. Even now he was bewildered.

"Younger Matthieu, Other, my poor boy," he whispered, "my poor boy…"

"Soon there will be just you and me. There will be no more light, just darkness. The feeling alone will remain with us — if you do not spurn it."

"Tell me what I should do!"

"Warmth…" said the youth, "come down here to me, touch me with your warmth! Do not think of the coldness which emanates from me! Kiss me on the mouth! I have still one joy to impart…"

"That is the wrong way," said Matthieu, "I will warm you, I will lie with you, but not for my benefit. You must be helped. I must think how I can help you. I must attempt the almost impossible."

"That is the wrong way. I shall not remain tepid flesh much longer. I stood on the street, cast out, ready for one last pleasure, but you spurned me. You accept nothing. My ugliness offends you. My youth does not help. My similarity to you is in vain. A single wound hinders this joy. It destroys this moment. It extinguishes us… Please don't forget, Matthieu, that you cannot live without me, without your own fifteenth or sixteenth year. You will be annihilated at twenty-five if you do not survive sixteen."

"My poor boy, I hear what you are saying. It conveys a sensible foolishness, but gets us nowhere. Your fever distorts reality. Believe me, we must reach a sober agreement, devise a plan so that this tomb will open up, the black town sink, and day return. A monstrous dimension has eliminated the orderly course of things; but such excesses cannot last long. Events, unhinged reality, will find their way back from the chaos. Nothing else will be real except that I have found you, and our mutual happiness."

A feverish gaze, alien, veiled, alighted on Matthieu. The latter shuddered, there was a storm raging within him; he believed that his young friend was already slipping over to the other side of the darkness. Yet the mouth beneath the eyes still moved.

"You forget the place that holds us. You do not want what I want. You are still dreaming of a world that has long since spat us out. We only have meaning for one another. The rooms we have left no longer exist. We are surrounded by total solitude, looking at one another in our nakedness with pity and revulsion and awaiting the ultimate: the irrationality of a desire, a demand born of love, the crime committed by one against the other. Why don't you want to be my murderer? What stops you? Why do you wish to entrust my death to this loveless disfigurement? There is nothing noble in dying of a sordid wound. Unleash your fury upon me, Matthieu! Tear me apart! Can there be any other joy in this tomb, in this place with nowhere adjoining it, than a murder which no one resists? It is already half completed. Why haggle over the other half?"

"My poor boy — those aren't your thoughts. Grief and despair are speaking through you. You seek unknown, imagined raptures, which, if they assail you, would be more bitter than anything else. Your wish is a betrayal of both you and me. The misery in which we find ourselves now orders you to step through a door which only opens once. No, no, I won't be the one who slams it behind you. We must not do anything irrevocable. We are not about to cast ourselves behind a hedgerow in order to throttle the life in us, scoundrels who return their shameful existence. Together we shall summon the power of our hearts and use it, even if we do not recognise the foe, our foe, the foe of our well-being."

Other made a grunting sound which Matthieu was unable to interpret. Worried, he looked down at the youth who lay motionless, at the wound which foolishly had been left untended. A coil of entrails, a grimy bubble, stirred unprotected.

Matthieu, still confident a moment before, felt unable to meet the uncertain task with which he was faced. The power of his heart, which he had relied upon, did not match up to it. His feet were leaden. The young man's torment filled him with horror. Horror and a mysterious indecision. He spoke the youth's name once more. Once more the gaze of the other turned on him, some kind of gaze without focus.

"Young Matthieu... I shall hurry outside, cleanse my hands with snow and then attempt to treat the wound."

"You must not go outside. You cannot even do so," the youth answered firmly. "Your hands are clean enough to touch my wound. Even unwashed, they are cleaner than the gangrenous blood. Your urge to return my entrails to their place is driven by your belief in some dark obligation. But why? You are just being headstrong. In the end I must submit because you are the older. I shall keep still."

"Whatever I do will be reckless," Matthieu sighed. He attempted to gather his wits with an almost unbearable effort; but a cold-blooded resistance in his brain thwarted his attempt. He still could not solve the paltry secret of this encounter, this hour, this place. The complicated apparatus made of flesh, blood, nerves, his body, his property in which he was encased, refused to obey. All he perceived were his trembling hands. He felt that dizziness occasioned by fear which precedes unfathomable dread. With a scarcely human resolve he began to speak once more, every word an act of defiance to his foundering consciousness. And it was merely a miserable recital of all that he could not be spared from doing.

"I shall... replace what has issued from your body. Please, do not scream too loud. Try not to move."

With less effort he added:

"We are as poor and naked as at birth — so bloody — and even more forsaken... Completely without succour."

Other did not answer. He squeezed his lips together tightly, evidently resolved to endure whatever might come. Matthieu, who read this behaviour in his own way — as a decision to continue to embrace existence, not shake it off like an early-ripening fruit — had to dispel yet another bout of inner abstraction. He had not guarded himself sufficiently against the exhaustion which increasingly gripped his being. It was as if he had forgotten that he existed in time. Seconds, minutes, hours perhaps, all had the same length or duration. A numbing, stifling slowness of his senses continuously erased the weight and sequence of this and every other adventure. His memory putrefied.

Now he knelt beside the sunken bed, extended his right hand to the wound, carefully groping in the air. Suddenly Other grabbed his arm with an unexpected movement, grasped it tight, stopped his movement in order to delay the inevitable pain. Or so, at least, Matthieu interpreted this sudden intervention.

"I shall be very careful, Other," he whispered.

The youth winced, tautened his lips till they were no more than a thin line, a tightly fastened slit.

Then Matthieu experienced a jolt. He saw nothing more. He fell forward, reaching with his free hand at first into emptiness; then supported himself — and the support he found came from the body of the youth who was lying somewhere beneath him.

In this moment, half sunken into the pit, he realises clearly, all too clearly, what has happened. The candle had burnt down; the last of the molten stearine had carried the wick down into the bottle-neck where it expired. Simultaneously — as if the onset of darkness had been the sign for which Other had been waiting — the youth thrust the arm he was clasping tightly down inside himself. The horror Matthieu experiences is beyond imagination, turns him to stone. For a moment he can do nothing but support himself. He notes that he is holding himself up on one of the youth's knees. Then he takes stock of his right hand.

It has plunged through the wound into the body. He had felt the resistance which the exceedingly narrow opening had presented to the mighty thrust. The youth's rage, his desire for death, ignored both the pain and the resilience of the flesh. This reversal of birth had gone unhindered.

His hand is immersed in the warm froth of entrails. Were Matthieu to reach into the darkness he would gain an experience, a certainty — laughably small in comparison with the vast horizons of his longings — but a certainty none the less: that one can crush a person's heart.

The horror, whose repugnance is beyond his powers of comparison, has made him neither wicked nor even foolhardy. He is no plunderer. His brain has frozen, his pulse stopped; but he does not yield to the calamity, does not plummet into the abyss. It feels as though his hand has slipped between the meshes of a net that were too narrow for such a hand. It is trapped. It is inside the inner space of a person, a youth whom he loves. It resembles that of a murderer. He must withdraw it. It cannot remain where it is. But every movement, the very attempt to extract it, fills the victim with raging pain. Matthieu hesitates. He listens in the darkness for some utterance from the other. The murderer awaits a movement, a cry, forceful opposition. But all that comes is a faint breath, almost a nothingness of a sound.

With great self-command, yet simultaneously revolted, Matthieu withdrew his hand. It slid, far more easily than he had expected, through the opening which proved to be elastic. He then clasped the knee joint once more with his left hand, assuring himself that the body had not been carried away into the darkness.

Matthieu straightened himself; but then bent forward again. The youth's silence was threatening, the sign of a degrading transformation...

His head was still there, the chest too, he was still there, the younger Matthieu, from his toes to the hair on his head... But he was sinking. Fifteen or sixteen fetching years were being snatched away, undone. A human form, the most beautiful that Matthieu would attain, was vanishing in the darkness, crumbling away or being withdrawn. The goal of its impassioned growth had been annulled.

Matthieu heard a groan whose timbre he recognised, the hollow groan of agony that had already half destroyed his consciousness. The youth's lips must have relaxed and opened. The sound he uttered was a deeper, softer howl than before, like a last statement.

Matthieu wanted to scream. He couldn't. Fear, until now constantly suppressed or thwarted by paltry hopes, had overwhelmed life. He surrendered to it with dull horror. He felt his brain sweat and this inner perspiration became a dissipating poison, an inner darkness corresponding to that surrounding him. And simultaneously a silence began to rage inside him, a tumult without sound. All of his beliefs, well-meaning, familiar reassurances born from his trust in life, obeyed him no more. The impalpable phantom, which had no valid name, had penetrated every cell of his body like a tangle of roots. Still he flailed in this net of flames, and suffered the revolting penetration that had destroyed him. He still breathed. He passed water. He soiled himself.

His gagged feelings, his spent yearnings, his charred joys gathered to form one single feeling of remorse, of futility, of abandonment. He no longer knows what he loved in the other; the sixteen years, his own self, the graceful figure, the scarcely corrupted hands, the mouth, which he had forgotten to kiss, the sex, a swooning for which there is no name... Had he ever loved, thrown himself at their feet? With one stroke of charcoal everything is made null and void. Without a past he stands facing the now hostile images whose repugnant colours have the dimensions of the stench, possessed of a physical fear, by the fear of his body whose screams have been stifled.

He just manages to register that he is walking, soaked through by the horror of death. He is just able to perceive the crash of the hatch. This sound, mightier than thunder, the blare of a thousand trumpets, like the roar of a splitting mountain, releases him once more from the embrace. Yes, he wipes the sweat from his brow and hair; he notes his soiled state with a kind of shame, speaks a few words of sense which admittedly he does not think through with total clarity, but which stem from the mechanisms of his mind:

"Other is dead. The coffin has closed. A devastating end."

He resolves to put on a bold front. He will flee. He will return to the outside. He will get out of this funeral vault at all costs. He begins to wander. He kicks over the bottle which had served as a candlestick. He stands with both feet on the hatch, beneath which lies the maimed corpse, stretched out, naked, not even wrapped in the bed covers. Matthieu's ribs extend; a painful, rattling sigh wrests itself from his chest. He feels the desire to weep; but his eyes remain dry. He taps his way along the wall. He wants to find the door. He does not find it. He continues groping with his hands. He walks back and forth. He sketches out the ground plan of the cellar, the four sides of the walls, in the blackness. He crawls across the floor. He cannot find the door. He doubts that it exists. Yes, it no more exists than the sixteen years which have now been wiped out. He looks for the last matches. He does not find them. He rummages through the pockets of the jacket and trousers which are lying somewhere on the floor. He does not find the matches. His hand lands on the blood-soaked rag which had covered Other's wound. Revolted, he throws it away, but his hands retain the odour of the blood and mucus. He does not find the matches. The darkness is unbearable. It is so close that it constricts his chest. Suddenly he says: "I can't go on. I am imprisoned. I am walled in."

With these words he at last surrenders himself to the fear that had slightly loosened its grip. The eyeless face presses against him. He flinches. He finds himself with his back to the wall. He stares into the blackness, into this extreme blackness in which he cannot exist. But it is also unable to absorb him, this pitch-black gravitation, this all-destroying unbirth. He would remain outside of it, hurled to the ground, frozen with an incomparable terror made flesh.

He rebelled for one last time. He spat at the night, to see whether his spittle would rebound from the wall of nothingness. He moved again, stamped on the boards of the hatch in the floor, called down the name of the other into the tomb, wished putrefaction on the corpse, yelled words of warped accusation, appealed in the name of his warmth, his blood, his flesh, his seed, his brain, his senses, his birth, his past — on behalf of all of this useless totality. His momentum tipped him into emptiness. He had lost the existence he had claimed to possess. His memory was annihilated by the wild madness of despair. He felt fear as if touched by a form. It stood barring his way. He had been poured into it; it was the mould for his being, his body. Some impulse ordered him to smash it, to dare to break through the fabric of his incarceration to leave the terror behind him as an empty husk.

He ran blindly forwards, stooped, head first. He tripped, shortly before his goal. The impact was hard. The pain was as great as a universe, but so brief that Matthieu did not even scream. He straightened himself in front of the wall, already completely free of the devastating dagger wounds to his skull. For a moment he felt something like absent-mindedness, as if he had opened a door through which he had no intention of passing — or as if he had woken up in his bed and had not immediately recognised his room because he had been lost in a dream.

Then he fell. He sensed himself topple. Yet however unavoidable the fall, it slowed down: gravity seemed to have been suspended. At the same time he realised: it was not the law that had been inverted; rather he was being upheld. The one who had turned from his side when he entered the town had returned.

Matthieu could not see him; but he was clinging gently to him. He felt his nakedness on that of the other. The beautiful, powerful chest which supported his back, the enveloping contact of the thighs, the hands, which sought his skin as if stroking it, the hint of a mouth which was close to his...

Without question the darkness that enclosed him and the other had a taste of helplessness.

Matthieu did not take in the hardness and coldness of the tiles. A hand, which scarcely belonged to him any more, glided back and forth along the ground as if searching. With a thick, heavy tongue he slurred:

"Gari — who I know — angel, dark angel — with curly hair — Malach Ha-Mavis — with full, ruby lips — my friend, who I know well — with curly hair — Gari — who I know…"

With extreme clarity he heard the lid crash down on to the walled-in grave.

Brief Autobiography

The person I wish to discuss is myself. For the sake of convenience and decency I shall state from the outset that like everyone, I advocate certain things that are not mine to advocate. My life has now lasted thirty-five years, so you can easily deduce all that must have been omitted from this handful of typewritten pages. The whole thing is nothing but a tissue of lies created by silence, which may only be taken for the truth because no description can ever be complete. Science is no different. According to my birth certificate I was born on 17 December 1894 in Altona-Stellingen. Until my nineteenth year I spent my youth solely in Stellingen, apart from a couple of excursions and the daily journey to school in Hamburg. For thirteen years I was shackled to the school regime: in terms of time, more than a third of my past life; in terms of their impact, a far greater mass of experience, to wit the fruitful and frightful years between thirteen and twenty. On wooden benches. With no escape.

At the age of fifteen I began to write literary works. I had not read any books, or at least very few. I had only an imperfect idea of what I was letting myself in for. My youthful philosophy commenced, as for everybody, with the theory of identity. I cornered everyone with brutal, adolescent conclusions that brooked no compromise. All I understood of philosophy was archaic. As I said, I had read little. Everything to me was like glass, transparent. I invented words and connections. During the rain of sounds I sometimes fell into a faint. These were clearly my first struggles with the consolidated majority. I totally misjudged my situation. At the age of seventeen I wrote a number of plays. The editors at the publishers S. Fischer encouraged me to continue. Which made me foolish enough to have hopes of a better future and for a while I regarded pen and paper as the most consummate inventions of the human mind. I made abundant use of them. It is impossible to give the exact number of works from my most productive years. The majority have been destroyed. At high school on Kaiser-Friedrich-Ufer I had to prepare for my school finals. I was no longer quick-witted, merely thorough. I was preoccupied with the harmonic and brutal events of the world. I was a Socialist, according to my understanding of the term. The last three tiresome years up to the finals were spent in intoxication, in rebellion, in flaunting regimes. The revenge wreaked by matter and environment was not petty, did not simply produce a third-rate pupil; their ideas, conclusions and indignation went the whole hog. I became piously Christian. I stopped lying. This decision brought disaster down on me. Impossible to describe the torments. Piety was cast overboard. I fled, wandered throughout northern Germany. With no future. Was fetched back. It hadn't been worth it: decimation of physical energies. Passed finals. Regimes remained as strong as ever.

Then came the World War. After three days I was a convinced pacifist.

Brief Autobiography

How, why? Not even then was I as totally stupid as some had assumed from my ponderous bearing. Perhaps already before the outbreak of war I had reached the conviction — amid the confusions of religious suffering and struggles — that given the development of technology in a predetermined direction (squandering manpower) humanity must adopt a different set of morals from those laid down by existing religious societies. It struck me as vainglorious to proclaim the commandment "thou shalt not kill", while allowing explosives to be manufactured and ewes to be whipped until they give birth prematurely to lambs as incense for well-to-do ladies.[1] I saw such actions as violations of life itself, which were bringing an end to the civilised races. I realised that humanity does not need regulations, external laws, conventions or corruption along the lines of "you scratch my back and I'll scratch yours", but instead an ethical commitment that allows for the fact that it is a mass, a mass of people. Along with this mass of people: the animals. Ramparts against mechanical devastation, against poison gas, against the ambition of individuals for whom annihilation was simply a means to ultimate ends. Against our lives being gobbled up by manufacturing processes that squander material and manpower. In autumn 1915 I travelled with my friend Harms to Norway. During the first weeks after our arrival I finished the play *Pastor Ephraim Magnus,* which was published three years later by S. Fischer and received the Kleist Prize. I am not shy to admit that even today I stand by this work and that it has qualities which are of slightly more value than cardboard. But let me recall

1. Jahnn is referring to the method for producing Persian lamb fur from lamb foetuses.

after a further decade of life — in which I have seen the pious and the righteous turn grey before pettiness and partiality, and that history, on the small and the grand scale, is nought but a painted whore, a tiny trifle, a rotting and malodorous rag — that while still very young and without faking a thing, I ventured slightly closer to Hell than the rabble that thought it was justified in tanning my hide.

Broad sections of Norwegian life are reflected in my novel *Perrudja*. I spent four years writing the first two volumes. I attempted to depict nature and the mechanism known as man. His anatomy, the way it everts itself to become both hideous reality and fairy tale. A simple course of events and improbability.

After the publication of these first volumes a lot of people recognised the labour that had gone into them, and praised them. The fact that it was almost impossible to find a publisher for the novel should not be overlooked. Its length and the singularity of the topic scared off even the boldest. Prior to *Perrudja* came not only *Pastor Ephraim Magnus* but also: *Hans Heinrich; The Coronation of Richard the Third; The Doctor, his Wife, his Son; The Stolen God; Medea;* along with many dozen essays, scientific treatises and reports on experiments. More recently a number of other dramatic works have appeared: *Street Corner; New Lübeck Dance of Death.* For a long time now the public has been able to access the stirrings of my existence but in place of autobiographical lies we have the untruths disseminated by rumour and critical opinion. The loudspeakers boom: Yesnoyesnoyesnogaga.

In 1916 I turned my mind to the theory of organ building. My chief interest became the field which may be summarised as the calculation for scaling the ranks of pipes. Together with Harms, from 1916 to 1923 I based the size of the pipes to be built on easily manageable mathematical ratios. The merit of this work on scaling is that the sound-image can be set down numerically in equations. By this means the overall body of sound generated by an organ is no longer a chance matter; rather it is firmly outlined by the functional and emission values of the pipe rows. Our work led to the discovery that every flue pipe, every musical instrument, has not only emission values based on intensity, but also accumulation values independent of these, based on the organ's power and precision. This discovery has proved to be of revolutionary significance for organ specifications across the whole of Europe.

As work progressed it became apparent that the connections between the accumulation values and the intermittent wave are not only of great importance for organs, but may also be destined to exert a telling effect on the rendering of sounds produced by membranes (gramophone, radio, sound film). I have not yet been able to complete these tasks, which are of the greatest economic importance. I have come to lack all the necessary resources — money, space and time.

I have devoted a great deal of effort to improving the construction of the "*Schleifen*" windchest[2] and re-establishing its use in organ building. Here too I have been successful.

2. Cf. Hans Henny Jahnn, *Der Einfluß der Schleifenwindlade auf die Tonbildung der Orgel*, Hamburg, Ugrino Verlag, 1931. [Trans.]

Incidentally, I am rarely offered work in Germany. Occasionally I am consulted abroad as a scientific advisor. My work is honoured in foreign manuals, whereas, in the confines of my homeland, every effort is made to deny my existence. Simply put: it was a great mistake not to keep my literary ventures incognito. An author of ill repute is unable to inspire trust in Church authorities. The organ industry, which for a while was against me, even hit on the idea of finding unseemly passages in my literary works and sending them to the ecclesiastical offices. It goes without saying that it was pointless for me even to attempt to adopt the motto: "I bear no resemblance to the rumours about me."

ATLAS PRESS

Eclectics & Heteroclites
Also published in this series:

1. Hermann Nitsch *on the metaphysics of aggression*
2. Jennifer Gough-Cooper & Jacques Caumont *Marcel Duchamp, A Life In Pictures*
3. Grayson Perry *Cycle of Violence*
4. (Henri Beauclair & Gabriel Vicaire) *The Deliquescences of Adoré Floupette*
5. Alice Becker-Ho & Guy Debord *A Game of War*
6. Konrad Bayer *the sixth sense* (illustrated by Günter Brus)
7. Michel Leiris *Mirror of Tauromachy* (illustrated by André Masson)
8. Carlo Emilio Gadda *The Philosophers' Madonna*
9. Louis-Ferdinand Céline *Semmelweis*
10. Georges Perec *Cantatrix sopranica L., Scientific Papers*
11. Norman Douglas *Some Limericks*
12. Raymond Roussel *The Dust of Suns*

*For the complete Atlas Press catalogue,
on-line ordering, and to sign on to our emailing list
giving details of future publications:*
www.atlaspress.co.uk